THE LITTLE BOOK OF
MG

Written by Jon Stroud

THE LITTLE BOOK OF
MG

This edition first published in the UK in 2007
By Green Umbrella Publishing

© Green Umbrella Publishing 2007

www.greenumbrella.co.uk

Publishers Jules Gammond & Vanessa Gardner

Printed and bound in China

ISBN-13: 978-1-905828-88-3

Contents

Introduction

WHEN WRITING THE LITTLE BOOK of MG, I suddenly became very aware of how many beautifully kept vehicles there were within a stone's throw of my own house. To my amazement I found that in this small Cotswold village, population 625, there are at least seven examples ranging from a beautifully restored 1933 J-type Midget through a selection of MBGs to a rather smart MG-TF. So what is it about this diminutive pocket racer that stimulates such interest amongst car enthusiasts the world over? The answer is quite simple. It is passion.

MG sports cars were always designed and built by engineers who understood that there was more to creating an exhilarating driving experience than simply fitting a powerful engine to a lightweight chassis. Unfortunately in this day and age that little extra something is harder and harder to come by with the graceful stroke of the designer's pencil replaced by hi-tech CAD-CAM technology and wind tunnel testing, and the oily fingered skill of the expert tuner sidelined in favour of the plug-and-play computerised technology of twenty-first century diagnostic systems. Whilst modern motors may be frighteningly efficient and crammed with more computing power than the space shuttle, they lack the passion and soul of a true classic – how many BMWs sitting on driveways today will still be in existence 30 or 40 years from now, let alone in the hands of their original owners?

ABOVE The MG octagon – a motoring icon

And that is the crux of the MG experience. An MG is not just about the steel, leather and walnut that combine to sculpt this beautiful car; it is more than the sum of its parts. Owning an MG opens up a love affair with the open road.

For every immaculately restored MG residing under a tailored dust-sheet within the confines of a temperature controlled garage, there are one hundred machines in varying states of repair that are used almost every day come rain, shine, fog, hail or snow, giving their owners countless miles of thrill-packed motoring delivered in unique style by what is undoubtedly Britain's best loved sports car. To borrow from the words of Albert Einstein, MG owners love to travel but hate to arrive!

Chapter 1

Morris Garages – The Birth of MG

TO TRACE THE ORIGINS OF BRITAIN'S favourite sports car it is necessary to take a look at the lives of two of the motor industry's greatest visionaries: William Morris and Cecil Kimber.

Born in Worcester on 10 October 1877, William Richard Morris was the son of Frederick Morris, a draper's apprentice originally from Oxford but recently returned from working in Canada, and Emily Ann, a farmer's daughter from the village of Headington (now part of the City of Oxford). At the age of three, William and his family returned to Oxfordshire with Frederick taking a job as bailiff on the family farm. As young William grew he attended the village school at nearby Cowley where his

brightness and ingenuity first became apparent. A keen interest in cycling provided a suitable outlet for his burgeoning mechanical skills whilst also allowing him to demonstrate his athletic abilities as an amateur racer. Despite his obvious talent for engineering it was the prospect of studying medicine that excited the adolescent Oxonian. Unfortunately Morris's youthful ambition was to be cut short when, just before his sixteenth birthday, his father was forced to give up work through illness. With no breadwinner in the household it was left to William to abandon his formal education and find a job.

Capitalising on his mechanical knowledge and love of bicycles he found

employment in a local cycle shop but soon left to set up business for himself. With just £4 as working capital he set up a workshop at the back of his parents' home in James Street and set to repairing cycles. Always the entrepreneur, it was not long before the business was able to expand allowing Morris not just to repair

bicycles but to build his own machines, with new premises being acquired on Oxford's High Street for sales and Queen's Lane for storage.

As the 1800s gave way to the twentieth century, Morris extended his business interests yet further by going into partnership with Joseph Cooper to build

ABOVE William Morris,
1st Viscount Nuffield,
1934

motorcycles, for which a workshop was found at Hollywell Street (now called Longwall Street) in the centre of Oxford. Cooper's faith in the project, however, was short-lived. Concerned at Morris's insistence on ordering engines in bulk to save costs and without orders, the partnership dissolved within months and Morris found himself in debt. This proved to be but a temporary setback as the well-engineered bicycles and motorcycles started to sell well to Oxford's army of sporting young undergraduates. With a large workshop now at his disposal Morris turned his hand to another fledgling market: the motor car.

In 1903, with another partnership quickly formed, the Oxford Automobile and Cycle Agency was born; his associates in this being wealthy undergraduate Launcelot Creyke and local businessman FG Barton. It was to be yet another short-lived enterprise. With Morris inex-tricably tied to the engineering aspects of the Agency, Creyke took on the role of marketing the venture. His spending was, however, completely out of proportion to the size of the business and within a year they were bankrupt. Not only was Morris left with a sizeable share of the trading liabilities he was also forced to repurchase his own tools at auction following the liquidation of the company. It was a huge lesson for the young entrepreneur, one that lead him to swear that never again would he share control of a business with others and that in future his resources would be ploughed into developing superior, cost saving production methods rather than investing in ill-conceived promotion and marketing.

A far from easy task, Morris set to rebuilding his business single-handed. With an eye for the future, he concentrated his efforts on motor cars: disposing of his High Street cycle trade in 1908 and forming WRM Garages in 1910. By this time he was referring to himself as a motor car engineer, agent and garage proprietor and was not only providing mechanical services and sales of, amongst others, Humber, Singer and Arrol Johnson cars but also driving tuition, taxi and hire services – unheard of in

Edwardian times. New buildings were erected the following year on what has become Longwall Street by his landlords, Merton College, whilst additional premises were acquired on Queen Street, St Cross Road and within the Clarendon Hotel, Cornmarket Street. The name above the door of each of these establishments was Morris Garages.

For many the ownership of a flourishing sales and servicing business such as this would have been ample in terms of venture and satisfaction but not so for Morris. The consummate engineer, he could not help but be frustrated by so many of the vehicles that he sold or repaired – these were, after all, still the pioneering years of automotive history. Convinced that he could do better, pen was put to paper and a new advanced design formulated.

With a new company name – WRM Motors Ltd – and production installed at the disused Military College in Cowley, a grand establishment purchased for the sum of £10,000, the first Morris Oxford rolled off the makeshift production line in April 1913. Priced at £165, this 8.9hp two-seater was an expensive car for the day. However with a high basic specification including many features traditionally considered to be expensive aftermarket accessories and exceptional reliability it was an instant hit showing favourably in the numerous trials and hill-climbs that were so popular with

ABOVE William Richard Morris, 1st Viscount Nuffield, writing his New Year's message, encouraging the war effort on the production lines

MORRIS GARAGES – THE BIRTH OF MG

motoring enthusiasts.

Morris continued to grow his business but the outbreak of war forced a temporary suspension in the manufacture of cars as the Cowley works were turned over to the making of munitions. Initially this period caused great financial strain for WRM Motors but, in 1916, a lucrative contract was won for the construction of a new type of naval mine sinker. After an initial production of 250 units the Oxford plant was soon outputting 2,000 per week. For his contribution to the war effort William Morris was awarded an OBE.

After the cessation of hostilities WRM Motors Ltd was placed into voluntary liquidation in July 1919 and a new company, Morris Motors Ltd, was formed to take control of its assets. Production continued with a new 11.9hp engine supplied by the French company Hotchkiss who had transferred their operations to Coventry during the war in fear of being overrun by German forces.

After an initial post-war boom period, the motor industry suffered as the national economic position changed in the early 1920s. Within a mere four months from September 1920, sales dropped from 276 cars to just 74 this at a time when the production line was manufacturing 240 cars per month. Morris bravely tried to weather the storm but by February 1921 the problem was so severe that he no longer had the space to store the unsold vehicles.

It was at this time he took the decision to slash prices and in a stroke the four-seater Morris Cowley was reduced by a phenomenal £100. His aim was to maintain production even if it meant operating at a loss but it had an even more remarkable effect. Within six months sales had risen to 361 cars per month, the accumulated stock was sold and all of Morris's debts and loans were paid off!

It was at this time that Cecil Kimber joined Morris Garages as sales manager

under general manager Edward Armstead after being head-hunted by Morris himself. The 33-year-old Londoner had established a strong reputation in the motor trade having first been employed as assistant to the chief designer of Sheffield-Simplex before moving to the Thames Ditton works of AC Cars in 1916 being unable to fight in the war due to a severe leg injury sustained in a motorcycle accident in 1910. In 1918 he moved to the Birmingham component supplier EG Wrigley who were well known for their transmission and steering assemblies and a supplier to WRM Motors. Kimber was encouraged to make a large personal financial investment with Wrigley however this was lost after a deal went sour with the manufacturer Angus-Sanderson, for whom Kimber had styled a radiator.

In a surprising turn of events and without warning Armstead resigned from his position March 1922. To the shock of everyone who knew him and without explanation he committed suicide just two weeks later by gassing himself. Although he was just 34 years old, Kimber was immediately promoted to the role of general manager – a position he took on with relish.

Having spent time conversing with many wealthy young undergraduates Kimber came to understand their thoughts and desires and concluded that if he were to produce a 5% better car he could charge 50% more for the privilege. He soon started designing his own custom bodywork that could be fitted to the standard chassis manufactured by Morris Motors for use in their Oxford and Cowley models. Initially he commissioned two bodies from Oxford coachbuilder Charles Raworth which were then fitted to the Morris running gear in a small mews workshop in Alfred Lane. Sold under the Morris Garages banner, these special models were more sporting in nature and appearance to their standard counterparts – so much so that Kimber felt able to charge a premium price of £350 for one of his Raworth-bodied motors whereas a standard Cowley could be purchased for half of that. Not surpris-

ingly the cars were somewhat slow to sell. An undeterred Kimber set to designing a new machine.

In 1924 Morris Motors launched a revised Oxford, the 14/28, featuring a new 13.9hp engine. Re-jacketed with stunning and sleek aluminium body panels built by Hughes of Birmingham and featuring flattened springs, raked steering and a triangulated windscreen, Cecil Kimber's creation, the MG Special 4-seater Sports as it was advertised, made its first appearance in the April edition of The Morris Owner priced at £395. Although many would argue that the Raworth-bodied vehicles were in fact the first of the marque, it was the 14/28 Super Sports, as the range became known, that was the first to be officially called an MG. A month later, in the May edition of the magazine, an advertisement appeared for the £350 "MG Super Sports Morris". This advert not only displayed a photograph of the two-seater roadster being driven by Kimber's wife Rene and the words "will climb the famous Porlock Hill at 25 miles per hour" but also a simple logo – the letters MG contained within an octagon. The legend was born.

Chapter 2

Old Number One

FOR MANY ENTHUSIASTS THERE is an indelible link between the MG marque and competitive motor sport – a connection instigated by Cecil Kimber himself.

At about the same time that the first 14/28 MG Super Sports were rolling off the production line, Kimber instructed the Longwall engineers to start work on modifying yet another standard Cowley chassis. His design was completely different to anything the Morris Garages team had previously tackled. The rear of the frame was cut away and replaced by new side members tailored to rise up and over the rear axle allowing for the fitment of semi-elliptical springs whilst braking was improved by the installation of a more powerful four-wheeled system usually reserved for the larger Morris Oxford. The standard Morris side-valve motor was abandoned in favour of a special, modified 11.9hp overhead-valve Hotchkiss engine designed for the Glasgow built Gilchrist. Enveloping this was a narrow, cigar-shaped body constructed by Carbodies of Coventry with its two seats positioned in an offset fashion to further reduce width and aid streamlining. Painted in a dark grey that would become synonymous with MG's experimental vehicles, the car was finally registered FC 7900 on 27 March 1925.

At first, Kimber's new machine was far from perfect – breaking its chassis on one of the first tests – but, as is always the case with experimental vehicles and racers, repairs and modifications were hastily carried out and

the car was pronounced fit for duty. The first major outing for FC 7900 took place over the Easter weekend of 1925 when Kimber and his friend Wilfrid Mathews, an insurance broker from Oxford, headed down to Cornwall for the Land's End Trial.

Motor trials, still popular in the UK, were at the height of their popularity in the 1920s and 30s. From standard specification roadsters with their showroom gleam to Heath Robinson hand-built specials and experimental works cars competing across asphalt roads and rutted tracks, fords, streams and the most vicious climbs in the nation, these

ABOVE Old Number One's unusual offset seating arrangement

events stood as the ultimate test of man and machine. Just to finish was achievement enough.

Starting as number 310, Kimber's machine took in the course with ease combining enviable reliability with a stunning turn of speed, ultimately qualifying for a gold medal. Interestingly, there were three other MGs entered for the 1925 Land's End trial, two of which also attained the gold medal standard – the third being ineligible for the result as it was driven by a travelling marshal – but it was FC 7900, later to become known as Old Number One, that was the first purpose-built racing MG.

Sold after the 1925 trial for £300 to Harry Turner of Stockport, Old Number One was re-purchased by the MG factory in 1932 and has since been restored to its former glory. It now resides as part of the Heritage Motor Collection at Gaydon, Warwickshire.

Chapter 3

The Flatnose Sports Tourers

WITH THE BULLNOSE MORRIS Oxfords and Cowleys starting to appear long in the tooth after 13 years in production, the decision was taken to offer a restyled machine for 1926. Whilst clearly overdue, the changes were to cause a headache for Kimber and his Morris Garages colleagues for this was no simple cosmetic makeover. The new flat radiator Morris was built around an entirely new chassis that was wider, heavier, and shorter in wheelbase to its ageing predecessor and that now swept up over the rear axle.

Not only was it necessary for Kimber to redesign the MG's bodywork from tip to tail, he had also invested heavily in the design and manufacture of numerous special components for his 14/28s which, in a stroke, were all but useless. Furthermore, as if to rub salt in the wounds, he realised that for all the additional work and tooling required, the resulting machine would in all probability be inferior in performance to the older model due to its significant increase in weight.

Enlisting the help of Hubert Charles, a young engineering graduate who would later become intrinsic to the success of the marque in the 1930s, and his own wife, Rene, Kimber worked day and night to develop the next generation of MG cars. Their modifications were

extensive to say the least.

The completely restyled bodywork lost many of the classic curves that had once made the 14/28 such a desirable machine for young motorists with sporting aspirations. The radiator was, like the redesigned Morris itself, flat in profile whilst the wings and running boards were fitted to the chassis separately from the main body. The hefty original steering gear was replaced with a state of the art Marles system and fitted with a substantial 17½" René Thomas-steering wheel and the rear shock absorbers replaced. Considering it substandard, Kimber ordered the redesign of the entire braking system but, for all its complexity, the modified system was little better than the Morris unit it replaced. Five-stud open wire wheels fitted with balloon tyres, a quieter exhaust and a higher final drive

ABOVE A 14/40 Super Sports Salonette

RIGHT A 1931
University Foursome
Drophead Coupe

ratio completed the performance package whilst a whole host of additional cosmetic modifications from streamlined sidelamps and running board mounted toolkit to a special lacquered machine-turned body finish gave the new MG an individualistic appeal.

If ever there was to be an iconic finishing touch to the design of a motor car it was to feature on the first MG 14/40 flatnose sports tourer. Fixed to the honeycomb of the radiator and resplendent in solid German silver were the stylised letters MG contained within their now unmistakable octagonal surround.

Declared a resounding success by the motoring press of the day, the new MG 14/40 Super Sports retailed at £340 for the open two-seater and £350 for the four-seat version whilst the closed body Salonette sold for a more substantial £475.

Space always seemed to be at a premium within William Morris's ever expanding automotive empire. Having already moved to the Bainton Road premises of the Morris Radiators Branch in 1925 more pressure came to bear on MG production and in 1926 additional sites were commandeered for the service department in Merton Street and for the painting and bodyshop in Leopold Street. For Kimber this was, understandably, a less than ideal situation with varying aspects of production spread across the city of Oxford so, in 1927 he took a brave step and approached Morris himself with a bold request: he wanted £10,000 to build a brand new factory exclusively for MG manufacturing in Cowley.

Fabric Saloon was announced. Based on the 14/40 this closed body saloon featured a fabric-covered wooden body built by Gordon England Coachbuilders. Whilst essentially the same as the Salonette the unconventional construction allowed a certain amount of flex within the body dramatically reducing the rattles associated with rigid closed body cars of the time. Although this particular model has largely been lost to the ravages of time, its spirit lives on thanks to the quirky name of a particular demonstrator that over a period of time became a factory runabout. Splattered with flecks of paint from the workshop it became known to locals as the owld speckled 'un. To commemorate the 50th anniversary of MG the Abingdon-based brewery Moorland created a special ale – Old Speckled Hen – affectionately named after the fabric-covered workhorse!

To his amazement and considerable relief the request was granted and, with a turn of speed seldom seen in the modern world, a new factory was constructed in just six months – albeit at an inflated price of some £16,000. Kimber and his team of employees moved into the Edmund Road site in September 1927.

A few short weeks later at the London Motor Show the MG Featherweight

Success on the factory floor was, much to the delight of racing enthusiast Kimber, echoed by success on the

track albeit from the most unlikely of places imaginable. On 30 October 1927 at the San Martin racetrack just outside of the Argentinean capital Buenos Aires, Alberto Sanchíz Cires piloted his four-seat MG 14/40 to victory over seven other finishers in a one-hour race organised to celebrate the crossing of the South Pacific by two French aviators. With an average speed of 62mph, this achievement – MG's inaugural motor racing triumph – would be the first of many to come!

It was a hugely important time for the MG marque. Just two months before moving into Edmund Road, Morris Garages had been registered in its own right as a limited company separate from Morris Motors Limited, further reinforcing its status towards becoming a truly independent manufacturer of automobiles. Then, in the spring of 1928, The MG Car Company (Proprietors: the Morris Garages Limited) was established and the octagon was here to stay.

This was the same octagon that would start to appear on MG models in every conceivable form. Not only did the radiator proudly display the familiar motif but soon the hub caps, pedals, ventilators, tool box and door handles were all fashioned with the MG logo. Even the dashboard displayed an array of clocks and gauges housed in octagonal surrounds. But the overemphasised use of the eight-sided badge was more than just window dressing or a designer's obsession; this was a conscious effort by Kimber and his associates to create a brand identity that would distance the marque from the oft held opinions of some motoring enthusiasts that MG cars were no more than modified Morris Cowleys and Oxfords.

Fate smiled on the MG factory early in 1928 with the arrival at Edmund Road of a fabric-bodied Morris Light Six – an ill-conceived machine renowned for its terrible chassis and appalling handling characteristics which was, however, blessed with a powerful 2468cc six-cylinder OHC engine.

Discarding almost everything except the motor, Kimber's engineers set to designing a new chassis worthy of carrying the big six. With parts roughly sketched using a makeshift plywood drawing board and rudimentary drafting tools, two prototypes were constructed. Fitted with five-stud MG wheels and a new radiator designed by

Kimber himself and Ron Goddard of the Morris Radiators Branch, the first ground-up MG, nicknamed the Quick Six, was presented to William Morris. With the stroke of a hand the new design was passed and production approved.

Appearing in public for the first time at the 1928 London Motor Show, the 18/80 MG Six as it was officially monikered, was a highly modified version of the original Quick Six test car. The six-cylinder motor now boasted twin carburettors and highly polished components. Gone were the standard five-stud wheels – replaced by Rudge-Whitworth racing wheels with centre locking spinners. Gone was the 14/40 bulkhead and instrumentation – in its place a stunning arrangement of Jaeger dials edged in chrome and mounted on a jet black panel. But this was not a case of all show and no go like so many other cars of the age.

With a top speed approaching 80mph and acceleration to match, the 18/80 was easily stealing itself into territory traditionally regarded as the hunting ground of Lagonda and Alvis. This was a stunning machine by anybody's reckoning and testament to the ambition and achievement of MG.

LEFT The 18/80 with its distinctive radiator that would set the style for many MGs to come

Midgets and Magnettes

IN ADDITION TO THE TRIED AND tested 14/40 and state of the art 18/80, a third car graced the inaugural MG stand at the 1928 London Motor Show (in previous years the fledgling marque had shared floor space with its larger, mainstream brother Morris Motors). Small, light and nimble this car was to bear a name that would forever be linked with the MG brand to this day. Resplendent in gleaming red paintwork, this car was the M-type Midget.

Uncannily echoing current circumstances, there was an ongoing trend in the late 1920s whereby more and more motorists were switching to vehicles of smaller, more economic engine capacity. However, at this time the motives for downsizing were less driven by green concerns and more by taxation and the desire to avoid it. The British government was applying road tax to motor cars based upon their "Treasury Rating" derived from the RAC formula horsepower – a mathematical formula that calculated a notional horsepower rating

based upon the diameter (bore) of the cylinders and their number – quite simply, the larger the engine, the greater the HP and the higher the tax. Compounding this was the decision by the government in 1928 to reintroduced duty on petrol, a tax previously abolished under the Finance Act 1919. At a rate of 4d per gallon this took the average price of a gallon of petrol to just over 18½d - a rise of almost 30% in the space of less than a year.

The Baby Car was in, as was being proved by Austin with their immensely successful 747cc four-cylinder side-valve powered Seven that, at 360kgs, was

solution to the question of what should power their diminutive tourer. The answer came in the form of an ingenious 847cc bevel driven OHC that had been developed by the Wolseley Motor Company, a bank-rupted rival manufacturer that William Morris had acquired from Barclays Bank in 1926. To the sur-prise of the Morris engi-neers this innovative little motor proved to be quite a beast; so much so that it was decided that before being fitted to their new car it would have to be detuned and reworked into some-thing more manageable for the average family motorist.

half the weight of Ford's iconic Model T but offered similar performance. William Morris, somewhat irked by his competitor's foresight, realised that there was no choice but to produce a small, economic car of his own.

With time of the essence it was decided to look within the Morris organisation for a simple and quick

Offered as a two-door fabric-bodied saloon at £135 and as a £125 four-seat tourer, Morris Motors' new baby car, the Morris Minor, was announced at the end of August 1928.

Keen to make the best of a new oppor-tunity in the Morris stable, Kimber rap-idly acquired an early prototype Minor chassis complete with an original

ABOVE The M-type Midget racing at Grinders Glade during the Inter-Varsity Motor Trial in 1925

Wolseley engine still in its full state of tune. His train of thought was simple; if Morris had considered it too powerful for their conservative customer base then this little motor would be just ideal for the would-be sporting motorists that characterised the MG brand.

By MG terms, the conversion from family hack to pocket sportster was fairly straightforward. The original Minor chassis was deemed fit for purpose with only the scantest of alterations being required. The suspension was lowered as was the norm but the original wire wheels were retained, albeit with the addition of smart hubcaps embossed with the now familiar octagonal logo. Bodywork was of plywood overstretched with fabric and attached to a lightweight ash frame fronted with a compact version of the impressive flat radiator fitted to the all new MG Six and finished with a pointed boat-like tail that added to the machine's sporting appeal and race-track looks.

For the London Motor Show two prototype Midgets were built. The original blue-painted machine was to serve as a demonstration model whilst a similar red vehicle acted as a static display model on the MG stand. The truth of the matter was that, due to the tight time constraints involved, there was not enough time to complete two working machines, the untampered engines being in desperately short supply having been modified for production of the Morris Minor. And so it was that the second Midget was sent to Olympia with its bonnet shut tight concealing a roomy space where the 847cc OHC should have lived.

Despite this hidden collusion, MG's new baby was an immediate hit with the press and the public. The Midget offered performance that in many respects bettered its MG 14/40 brother by a country mile; all this in a package that, at £175, cost about half as much and little more than its basic Morris

Minor cousin. This was the 1920s equivalent of sticking a GTi badge and spoiler on the back of an unassuming family hatchback.

Although production of the Midget was unable to commence immediately the motoring public were literally queuing up to order this new breed of miniature sports car. Even Cecil Kimber could not have imagined the success that his MG brand would enjoy over the following year. Output had trebled with the Midget accounting for nearly 60% of production at Edmund Road – almost double that of the 18/80 MG Six which itself had undergone a transformation to the Mark II taking on a new, heavier chassis – the first created exclusively for an MG and not a Morris. Just two years after moving into the all-new, custom built Edmund Road factory the blossoming marque had outgrown its home. Another move was required fast!

LEFT At the MG factory at Abingdon, two MGs are sent down the line to the next stage of production, whilst mechanics are busy at work on other cars

Perhaps to reinforce the business's identity as a truly independent organisation, separate from Morris Motors in every respect, a new site for the MG Car Company was found away from Cowley at nearby Abingdon in a disused factory acquired from the Pavlova Leather Company, until recently one of the town's largest employers. With the move planned for January 1930 this bustling

RIGHT The huge MG 18/100 Tigress

market town eight miles south of Oxford and nestled on the banks of the River Thames would have been a breath of fresh air compared to the fast industrialising Oxonian suburbs.

Things were once again moving fast at the MG works and that included the cars as work had started on something special. Kimber made no secret of his desires for racing success and perhaps inspired by the Le Mans achievements of Bentley's Speed Six and 4½ litre machines (they had taken a clean sweep of the first four places and the Biennial Cup) ordered the creation of a pure bred racer based upon the 18/80. Extensive engine work was carried out incorporating a cross-flow cylinder head and the redesign of the crankshaft, pistons and camshaft. Suspension was stiffened with the fitment of a supplementary pair of rear shock-absorbers. To all of this was added a leviathan of a body. Designated the MG Six Sports Road Racing Model the impressive cream and brown racer later became known as the 18/100 Tigress.

The first object of Kimber's ambition was the Brooklands Double Twelve. Held in mid

May on the Surrey track's enormous 2.5 mile banked circuit, the Double Twelve was an endurance race run over two 12-hour legs on consecutive days which, in the 1920s, was considered as major an event in the social calendar as the Ascot Races or Henley Regatta. As the race grew close Kimber was approached by two friends, Randall and Edmondson, who were keen to enter three Midgets for the Double Twelve team prize. Inspired by their enthusiasm Kimber set his chief engine guru, Reg Jackson, the task of getting the most out of the tiny Midget power plant. Each internal component was hand polished by Jackson to a mirror finish using Shinio polish, a product similar to Brasso, whilst Hubert Charles, now head of design and development, increased power by an astounding 35% using his intuitive engineering skills to perfect the valve timing.

Five Midgets were specially prepared for the 1930 Double Twelve. Each featuring a specially tuned motor and benefiting from the addition of an extended range fuel tank, modified exhaust and racing bodywork complete with low cut doors. Three of the cars were destined for the Edmondson and

Randall team, known as The Tomato Growers due to the pair's market gardening business interests, the other two cars were for private owners who themselves had been inspired to take on the might of Brooklands.

Come race day the Tigress took off at a blistering pace lapping constantly at a thundering 86mph in the hands of

ABOVE The 1930 Double 12 gets underway

Howard Parker and Leslie Callingham. But, after just two hours of racing the big 18/100's motor expired in a cloud of smoke as the entire set of crankshaft bearings disintegrated and the engine seized. The mighty Midgets, however, fared considerably better. Finishing in 14th place with an overall distance of 1445.63 miles was the M-type of Randall and Montgomery who completed the event at an average speed of 60.23mph to lead home The Tomato Growers to team victory. The four other factory prepared MG Midgets all successfully crossed the finish line that afternoon taking 17th, 18th, 19th and 20th places, proving without a doubt the resilience and endurance of the

Mr Stisted and his mechanic making repairs to their MG during the British Double Twelve race at Brooklands

tiny lightweight sportster.

Alas, the poor competition performance of the 18/100 effectively signed its own death warrant; that and the hefty £895 price tag that took the heavyweight MG racer into the territory occupied by Bentley and Lagonda so production was ceased after just five machines had been manufactured. The Midget, however,

went from strength to strength with the improved valve timing of the Double Twelve racers now provided within the standard motor, its competition success reinforced by a strong showing in the Monte Carlo Rally at the hands of FM Montgomery.

Development of the Midget continued in the form of a new prototype, the

ABOVE British motor racing driver Cyril Paul talking about the success of his MG Midget racing car with his colleagues

EX120 (from this time all of MG's experimental vehicles were to be pre-fixed "EX"). Inspired by the design of an 1100cc French-built sports car, the MG engineers developed a chassis that, for the first time, passed underneath rather than over the rear axle allowing the car to take on a much lower centre of gravity and more aerodynamic profile. With square section metal tubing considered too costly and complicated to work with, a solution was found in the use of mild steel bicycle tubing brazed into custom turned brackets. This chassis was, in effect, a giant cycle frame!

Although Kimber had ordered the development of the EX120 chassis with the next generation of production

MGs in mind, a meeting with record breaking drivers Captain George Eyston and Ernest Eldridge soon set his thoughts to other uses. The two had set their sights on the Class H Hour Record for cars of less than 750cc and had been impressed with the competi-

tion performance of the diminutive Midget. Kimber offered the services of the MG workshops and the EX120 chassis assigning Reg Jackson, who had previously worked wonders on the Double Twelve engines, to labour full-time on the project under the

BELOW Captain George Eyston – Record Breaker

watchful eye of Eldridge.

With the EX120 chassis wrapped in a body vaguely resembling a low slung M-type and its highly tuned engine bearing little resemblance to the original motor the record car was taken to the grand banked "Piste de Vitesse" at Montlhéry, an oval track to the south of Paris.

Within a month the MG team were back at Montlhéry with the EX120. Having heard that Malcolm Campbell was to attempt the 100mph mark at Daytona in a 750cc Austin Seven, Kimber had insisted that the record must first be taken by MG. With the Eldridge engine repaired, tuned and now fitted with a Powerplus supercharger Eyston took to the track again. It was a huge improvement on their previous attempt but after constantly lapping at 97mph it seemed as if nothing could be done to crack the magic ton. Then an idea came from Jackson. If they could

streamline the frontal area of the car then it might just be enough to take the record. But they were at a remote racing circuit south of Paris and the MG workshops were hundreds of miles and a sea-crossing away. Showing the resourcefulness for which all of the MG team had become known, Jackson set to

ABOVE The EX120 testing at Brooklands

building a frontal cowl at the trackside from an old oil drum by first beating it flat and then forming it around a concrete drainage culvert. Heath Robinson it may have been but it was nonetheless effective and on the evening of 16 February 1931 four runs were achieved with a maximum speed of 103.13mph.

Hot on the record breaking success of the EX120 Kimber quickly announced the launch of yet another new produc-

tion machine – the C-type, or Montlhéry Midget. Priced at £345 in supercharged form or £50 less in "standard" trim, this car was not for the fainthearted and was sold as a road-ready racing car with centre lock wheels, racing exhaust and two-seater doorless racing bodywork complete with streamlined nose cowling, albeit not one made from an oil drum battered over a drainage culvert! The power-plant, a redesigned 746cc version of the M-type's four-cylinder OHC, produced a healthy 52bhp in blown form – almost double that of the standard Midget.

Fourteen machines were built and prepared in just 14 days ahead of the 1931 Brooklands Double Twelve and shipped just in time for practice. With the entire 200-strong MG workforce present, the Montlhéry Midgets performed remarkably by finishing seven cars and taking the first five places overall.

The winning car, driven by the Earl of March and Fairy Aircraft Company chief test pilot Chris Staniland, completed 1575 miles at an average speed of 65.62mph. Not surprisingly, MG was the proud winner of the coveted team award.

Whereas the success of the C-type Midgets was undoubtedly down to sound engineering principles, tenacious driving and downright hard work, the

demise of the EX120 can only be described as a cruel twist of fate and sheer bad luck. George Eyston had returned to Montlhéry to attempt yet another record – 100 miles in one hour. Testament to the work of the MG mechanics the special was now consid-

ABOVE Montlhéry C-type Midget

BELOW The C-type
Midget was described
as 'the fastest and
finest 750cc car money
can buy'

ered capable of this level of intense running; a feat which, just a few short months before, would have been considered impossible. Utilising the wide

banked circuit Eyston charged around without a fault until, after 58 minutes of driving, the waiting support team heard a change in the note of the exhaust as

BELOW The C-type Midget was described as 'the fastest and finest 750cc car money can buy'

EX120 sped past the pits. Determined to crack the record, he flashed passed his supporters yet again but missed the signal indicating that he had in fact completed the time and distance. Unaware of his error he charged on to complete another lap, waving to his crew as he crossed the finish line victorious – all that was left to complete was one complementary warm down lap. As the MG mechanics waited they suddenly became aware that the track had gone quiet. Leaping into their support car they set off around the track themselves and on rounding the first bend were presented with the site of EX120 aflame.

Worried that the heftily built Eyston might be trapped within the wreckage they approached the site at speed only to find he was not there. After a search of the area the bemused team returned to the pits to be told that Eyston, having felt flames around his feet had climbed onto the back of the car and bailed out at 60mph leaving EX120 to its own fate. As he did so he was spotted by the driver of a Citroen that was also testing on the Montlhéry track who stopped and bundled him into the car before heading off to the local hospital. Eyston thankfully recovered from his injuries but alas EX120 was no more.

With its sporting reputation building fast, MG announced two new models for 1932. The first of these, the D-type Midget, utilised a chassis based on that derived from the EX120 and Montlhéry Midget. To this, the reliable 847cc OHC motor of the M-type was fitted along with racing style centre-lock wheels, half elliptical springs and a three-speed gearbox. The second machine was designated the F-type. However, with its 1271cc six-cylinder motor and 10" longer chassis this was no baby car. Christened the Magna it was set to represent a new page in the history of the MG marque.

The reality was somewhat different. The exciting new engine was, in fact, no more that an M-type motor to which two more cylinders had been added – its

true identity being the power unit of the Wolseley Hornet. With just 37bhp on tap it was sorely underpowered and hardly represented the trademark speed and agility for which the Abingdon cars were becoming renowned. Nevertheless, the pretty looking car sold steadily priced at £250 for the open tourer and £289 as a closed salonette.

Over the following year, with a fall in sales and a realisation that MG's range of production cars was failing to keep up with the technology and reputation bestowed on their racing machines, Kimber ordered the design of yet another new model. He knew that through MG racing and record breaking endeavours the MG mechanics had the 847cc OHC in such a high state of tune that it was now producing almost double its original power output even without the assistance of a supercharger. He was also aware that the development of EX120, its successor EX127 and the C-type Midget had produced a versatile and capable chassis arrangement. It seemed obvious that the solution to MG's problem was to marry the two in an exciting new package.

The result was the J-type Midget. Offered as an open two-seater for £199 10s it cost little more that the M-type it replaced. For £20 more an open four-seater was available whilst £255 would purchase a salonette. Each of these machines featured the 847cc OHC with twin SU carburettors, now tuned to produce 36bhp, centre-lock wire wheels and a four-speed transmission. For those customers in search of something sportier still, two additional models were offered: the blisteringly fast super-charged J3 and the even faster J4 Racing Model. Utilising the Montlhéry-

developed 746cc OHC motor, both of these machines quickly developed a reputation for speed – too much speed. So much so that few drivers were brave enough to take on the ferocious J4 and those that did often ended up with hefty crash repair bills.

Also on display at the London Motor Show was another new model. Powered

BELOW The MG Magna and Midget being prepared for the 1932 Olympia Motor Show

ABOVE 1933-34 L-type Magna

by a triple SU carburetted 1087cc six-cylinder OHC developed from the F-type Magna, the K-type Magnette was first offered as a pillarless saloon with a costly price tag of £445 – over twice that of the J-type Midget and a £100 more than the larger 1271cc Magna. Despite

this latest incarnation of the octagon marque, incorporating improved steering and brakes and the option of a four-speed manual or pre-selector gearbox and the fact that it was later offered as a long chassis four-seat tourer and saloon, it proved difficult to sell to a sceptical

only 200 machines were manufactured.

A new Magna, the L-type, was announced in the spring of 1933. Developed from the F-type it featured a slightly modified wheelbase and similar bodywork – albeit with longer swept back wings that improved the car's looks considerably – but more crucially the 1087cc twin-carb OHC with four-speed gearbox of the K-type Magnette. Despite giving away 184cc, the MG-designed engine delivered an increase of 4bhp over its Wolseley derived counterpart. With prices varying between £285 for a two-seat roadster and £345 for the salonette, this new automobile was considerably more expensive than its predecessor; it was, however, a greatly improved car.

At this time it was becoming apparent to William Morris that, despite having trimmed the range from 16 models in 1932 to just 10 in 1933, MG expenditure on production and racing far outweighed what could be sustained. Kimber was forced to agree that in future more parts would be bought and acquired from within the Morris empire; the first step of which would be the dissolution of MG's long term relationship with Carbodies. Work commenced on

public. Even the coveted Mille Miglia team prize and a victory in the 1933 Ulster TT for the great Tazio Nuvolari at the wheel of what is often considered the greatest racing MG of all time – the specially prepared 120bhp K3 Magnette – could not sway opinion and in total

redesigning the faithful Magnette and popular Midget and by the close of the year the final J-type rolled off the production line soon followed by the last ever Magna.

Announced early the following spring, the P-type Midget was an altogether more modern car than those previously produced by the marque. Although the capacity of the four-cylinder OHC remained at 847cc, the motor itself had undergone a complete redesign and now featured three camshaft bearings which, although delivering marginally less power than the J-type, combined with an improved gearbox and clutch to offer far smoother running. Added to this was a substantially better braking system, stronger chassis and slightly more capacious interior. Priced at £220 it cost little more than its predecessor.

Launched simultaneously to the new Midget was a redesigned Magnette. The N-type made use of a substantially modified version of the "KD" designated 1271cc motor that had by this time become standard fitment on the K-type with drive provided via a four-speed manual gearbox. A tapered chassis and rubber mounted bodywork

(from the Morris Bodies Branch) added considerably to the comfort and handling. In addition to the two and four-seater models initially offered by the factory at £305 and £335 respectively, a

number of especially coachworked versions were made available, the most famous of which was the thoroughly gorgeous HW Allingham fastback bodied Airline Coupé.

But whilst it seemed to all that the Abingdon works had taken a huge step forward into the modern world there were dark and unforeseen clouds on the horizon that would change MG forever.

Chapter 5

A Time of Change

THE YEAR 1934 WENT WELL FOR Cecil Kimber and the MG marque. Whilst the road cars sold steadily the factory racers racked up win after win in spectacular fashion.

As the astounding K3 Magnettes continued to prove their worth with victories the world over, the new Q-type Midget racing model, powered by a tuned 746cc Zoller supercharged P-type engine, turned heads on domestic shores with a string of race wins for the works-backed Cream Crackers trials team (so called because of their distinctive cream and brown livery) and an astonishing 79.88mph standing start mile at Brooklands. The icing on the cake for the Abingdon racers and record breakers was delivered by George Eyston with a 128.69mph flying mile and 120.88 mile hour driving MG's latest experimental car, the EX135.

Many expected 1935 to be yet another opportunity for MG to fill their trophy cabinet with the spoils of a four-wheeled war of attrition. Indeed, by the middle of the year this seemed all the more probable, the company having just launched their inaugural single-seat production racer: the R-type Midget. Described at the time as "a genuine Grand Prix racing car in miniature" it featured the screaming supercharged 750 of the Q-type fitted to an all-new narrow chassis which, for the first time, utilised fully independent four-wheel suspension and a four-speed pre-selector gearbox.

Then an announcement was made that shocked the racing world to its core: the MG Car Company was to retire from competitive motorsport with immediate effect. A statement explained how MG had been effectively

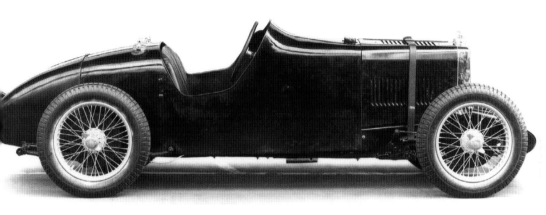

forced out of competition by unfair handicapping and that now was a time to concentrate on making use of the advanced racing-developed technology within their range of road cars. Subsequent accounts have proved these reasons to be far from the truth.

In recognition of his contribution to industry, William Morris had been raised to the peerage in 1934. Now titled Lord Nuffield he made the decision to amalgamate all of his businesses into a single group with the intention of making Ordinary shares available to the public. In 1935, under his direction, Morris Motors set about purchasing the SU Carburettor Company, Wolseley Motors, Morris Commercial, Morris Industrial and The MG Car Company leaving only Morris Garages and the Wolseley Aero Engine Company untouched. This new automotive super-company was named the Nuffield Organisation.

With the Morris takeover came great change. In an instant the MG design office was shut down, its staff made redundant with the exception of HN Charles who found himself transferred to the Morris Motors Cowley plant but the greatest shock for the Abingdon workforce was still to come. Nuffield

his first tour of the plant, he took one look at the racing workshop and exclaimed, "Well, that bloody lot can go for a start!" A single sentence had signalled the end of the MG racing legacy.

Lord insisted that he wanted to see an end to sports car development and demanded in its place a new saloon car. However Kimber, never one to play straight by somebody else's rules, formulated a design that in his mind offered a compromise – the SA. With an enormous 10ft 3in wheelbase this was like nothing MG had ever produced before. Powered by a six-cylinder 2288cc pushrod OHV this was a powerful luxury sports tourer. Although its size, absence of centre-locking wheels and lacklustre performance set it apart from previous MGs it was nevertheless a handsome gentleman's car with long sweeping wings and elegant bodywork echoing the art deco fashions of the moment. Priced at £375 it proved excellent value for money being almost

was concerned that Kimber was over-stretching resources and decided to act by demoting him to general manager and director, appointing Leonard Lord as managing director in his place.

It was obvious from the outset that Lord had no passion for sports cars and even less for what the MG brand had come to stand for. He was of a new breed of hardnosed hard-line businessmen for whom the bottom line was the be all and end all. His level of popularity within the Abingdon factory was secured when, on

£25 cheaper than the Magnette it would soon replace. Thankfully the marque's sporting image was maintained by the continued sale of the P-type Midget with its OHC now bored out to 939cc. However, this machine also found itself relegated to the history books with the announcement in 1936 of its exciting new replacement.

After considerable debate and to the relief of enthusiasts across the land, Kimber finally convinced Lord that MG needed to produce a new sports car. Whilst following in the spirit of previous incarnations of the Midget this machine was an altogether different beast. Built around a new chassis that was both wider and longer than before, the TA Midget was noticeably larger and roomier than before allowing more space for luggage and a bigger fuel tank – ideal for those fashionable weekend jaunts away. Powered by the smooth 1292cc four-cylinder pushrod OHV originally found lurking under the bonnet of

the Morris Ten and fitted with hydraulic brakes, softer suspension and a quieter exhaust, this new car was easier and more relaxing to drive. For the die-hard enthusiasts this was far from ideal! MG drivers liked their cars rough at the edges with a race track feel; this capacious sportster was far more refined. However, many were soon won over by its good looks, superb ride and £269 10s price tag.

The launch of the TA coincided with

BELOW 1936-1939 TA-TB Midget

yet another boardroom shake up at MG however, this time the outlook appeared far rosier for the Abingdon works. After less than a year in charge Lord was on his way having demanded an enormous increase in salary and a share in the Nuffield Organisation profits and been flatly turned down. On leaving, his responsibilities were passed to Oliver Boden but he in turn quickly moved on having been appointed group chairman. By the close of the year it seemed like it was business as usual as once again Cecil Kimber found himself back in control of the company he loved so dearly.

New for 1937 was the VA, a similar machine to the luxurious SA but with a shorter wheelbase and smaller engine. Intended to replace the now discontinued Magnette, it was powered by a twin carburettor 1548cc four-cylinder pushrod OHV similar to that used in the Wolseley Twelve and available as an open four-seater, saloon or Tickford drophead coupé. However, glamorous as it looked it was badly let down by its poor performance. Although at 54bhp the 1½ litre compact sports tourer boasted a similar power output to the Magnette it weighed substantially more and offered torturously weak acceleration.

Perhaps MG's most stunning venture into the world of luxury motoring came in 1938. With sales of the SA and SV showing promising numbers Kimber ordered the development and production of the WA. At 10ft 3ins it boasted the same wheelbase as its SA cousin but with advertising boasting "Capacious Coachwork", its 4ft 9in track was consid-

grand touring. Like its stablemates, acceleration was far from being a strong point but with the ability for effortless high-speed cruising at low rev it was a dream to drive and was rightfully considered a noteworthy alternative to the best luxury cars of the day.

Launched in May 1939 the TB Midget was to enjoy a relatively short production life as once again storm clouds gathered across Europe. Developed from the TA, this final pre-war embodiment of the Midget featured a modified 1250cc version of the Morris Ten motor which, thanks to a wider bore and shorter stroke, produced slightly more power than the 1292cc unit housed in the TA. A mere 379 TBs were produced before Cecil Kimber decided to suspend production at the outbreak of World War Two; little did he know that it would be the last car he would ever build.

erably wider. Similarities with the SA extended under the bonnet – the cruiser-like WA utilising a bored out version of its six-cylinder push-rod motor and now displacing 2561cc and generating 100bhp. The interior offered a stylishly redesigned dash with the usual plethora of octagonal motifs adorning every detail. This was a grand car for

Chapter 6

The Record Breakers

ALTHOUGH THE 1930S WERE troubled times for Cecil Kimber and the MG Car Company it was a period of remarkable development that saw record after countless record fall to a band of intrepid and fearless racing drivers.

George Eyston's destroyed EX120 had been replaced by its successor, the EX127. Known as the Magic Midget this was yet another pocket rocket that would appear on the scene to break speed records with regular monotony. The use of an asymmetric rear axle meant that the transmission could be mounted to one side which in turn allowed the driver to sit lower in the car adding to the streamlining effect and lowering the centre of gravity. On his first outing in the car Eyston recorded 114.77mph.

It was not just the Abingdon factory that was starting to produce record-breaking MGs. Other top drivers were taking on the might of the racing world with their own specially modified machines. One such driver was Ronnie Horton who developed a modified C-type with a similar offset transmission enveloped by a pencil-thin single-seat lightweight Jensen body. Against all odds this remarkable machine annihilated the opposition at the 1932 Brooklands 500 taking the outright win at an astonishing 96.29mph, having previously set a new Outer Circuit record of 115.29mph.

The following year saw the Magic Midget re-bodied and ready to once again attack the record books. However, in this new guise it was now too small for the tall and stocky Eyston to fit

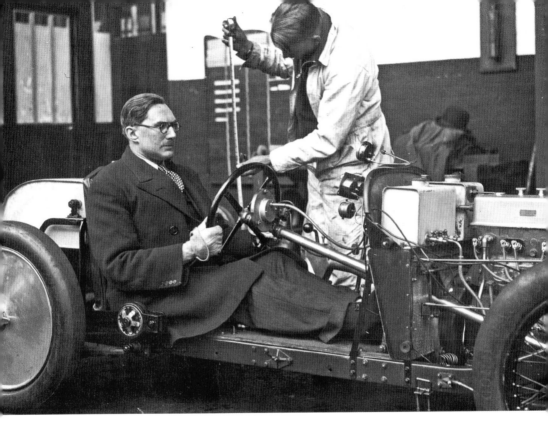

inside! An unlikely replacement was found in the somewhat smaller Bert Denly – Eyston's mechanic. With the scene set at the Montlhéry track and the amateur racer squeezed inside, EX127 set off round the "Grand Vitesse" to set a new record of 110.87 miles in the hour with a 128.63mph flying mile.

Horton, meanwhile, was developing a new racing machine of his own based on a standard road-going K3 Magnette two-seater, once again fitted with an off-set single-seat body. This new machine with its 1083cc engine pushed the

ABOVE George Eyston is measured at the wheel of the MG chassis which he would use to attempt a new world record at Pendine Sands

THE LITTLE BOOK OF MG 55

Brooklands Outer Circuit record first to 117.74mph before bettering it some few weeks later with a new mark of 125.58mph. This was all an impressive sight for the folk of the MG works but they knew that they too had a new and formidable track weapon – the EX135.

Built for Eyston and similarly constructed on a K3 chassis with an EX127-style asymmetric rear axle and offset transmission, the EX135 could be fitted with a choice of bodies dependent on the type of event being contested – one being for road racing and the other for

track events and record breaking. In what must have seemed like an identity crisis, the car was first known inevitably as the Magic Magnette however, as soon as it was seen in public in its road-racing form it donned a new and rather less mystic nom de plume – the Coal Scuttle! A more friendly identity was found when painted in its track guise of brown and cream stripes (the MG factory colours) and it soon took on the nickname of the Humbug. EX135 soon proved its worth with an outright victory in the Empire Trophy and a new hour record of 120.88mph at Montlhéry. However, with the suspension of Abingdon's racing ventures at the hands of Len Lord, it was sold to Donald Letts, a driver for the Bellevue team and a member of the famous diary manufacturing family.

1936 saw Horton's amazing offset K3 change hands too; the car having been purchased by sportsman, racer and all round good-egg Major Goldie Gardner. In his first outing at Brooklands he set a new Outer Circuit class record of 124.4mph, a mark which, due to the closure of the circuit at the outbreak of World War Two, stands to this day. Later that year, further modifications were made to the K3's engine by MG's Reg Jackson and race-tuning expert Robin Jackson. This included the fitment of a Zoller supercharger and a specially made bronze cylinder head similar to one that had been used by the record breaker Bobbie Kohlrausch. Gardner's record-breaking achievements in the Horton K3 culminated in a blistering 148.8mph flying kilometre on a stretch of as yet unopened autobahn near Frankfurt. Impressed with the performance of the quirky but effective British racer, Auto Unions chief engineer, Eberan von Eberhorst, approached Gardner and suggested that it was about time they fitted his car with an all-enveloping streamlined body. Kimber, his interest stimulated by Goldie's remarkable performance agreed and set off to approach his boss, Lord Nuffield.

To Kimber's delight, Nuffield agreed; the company was, after all, back on a level footing with the introduction of the new luxury sports tourers and there was no doubting in his mind that the publicity and profile generated by the record-breaking cars was good for the marque. Just as important was the fact that, compared to funding a full blown works team, racing against the clock was a relatively cheap form of motorsport.

The original intention of re-jacketing the Horton K3 was, however, soon scrapped. Kimber knew that a far superior chassis already existed and, what's more, it was fitted with an asymmetric rear axle and offset transmission. This was, of course, Eyston's original EX135. Within weeks money was exchanged and the Magic Magnette was returned home to Abingdon. MG's Reg Jackson and Syd Enever continued to develop Gardner's record-breaking engine with assistance from Robin Jackson with further modifications including the replacement of the Zoller supercharger with a newer Centric model whose function better suited the characteristics of the little 1083cc MG engine. In July 1938, with the reworked engine mounted to the EX135 chassis and fitted with a sleek low-profile body designed by Reid Railton, the car was presented to the press.

That November the new EX135 was

taken for its first true test as once again the Frankfurt autobahn and Speed Week beckoned. Gardner clocked a staggering 187.61mph for the flying mile, a figure which, despite being so fast, belied the true capabilities of the car – having made its return run at almost 196mph. The decision was taken that, with 200mph so tantalisingly close, another attempt should be made. The following June, once again on the Frankfurt autobahn, another attempt was made.

The figures were once again beyond belief as the mile was taken at 203.9mph, the kilometre at 203.5mph and the five kilometres at 197.5mph. But this, the Class G 1100cc record, was not enough for the MG crew and they set to stripping the engine at the roadside. Jackson and Enever carried out the amazing task of boring out the engine by 20 thou to take the capacity to 1,106cc thus making

EX135 eligible at Class H for 1500cc machines. With the motor reassembled Goldie Gardner set out once again for his high speed passes recording an identical 203.9mph for the mile but increasing the kilometre to 204.3mph and the five kilometres to an incredible 200.6mph.

One would probably expect the onset of war to put paid to any further record attempts with EX135. It certainly put further plans on hold but time would show that there would still be life in the old dog yet.

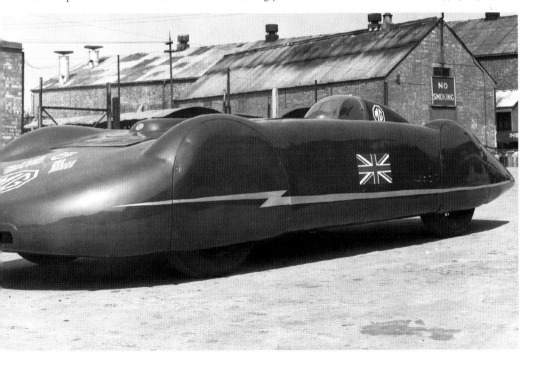

Chapter 7

Abingdon at War

MG'S CAR PRODUCTION may have been suspended in 1939 with the onset of hostilities between Britain and Germany but the Abingdon works remained far from dormant. As soon as the last completed cars were being shipped out of the finishing shop Kimber and his associate George Propert went looking for War Department contracts. With a reputation for superlative engineering it was not long before the first of these was issued for the construction of shell racks - a process which well utilised the factory's press shop. Soon larger and more significant jobs were awarded including the overhaul of Carden-Lloyd

and Matilda tanks although the excitement of being awarded a contract for the reconditioning of Browning machine guns for the fabled Spitfire fighter aircraft turned to bitter disappointment when it was pointed out that without a firing range they would not be able to undertake the work.

Work then moved to the repair of armoured cars and the assembly of lorries shipped from the United States in kit form. A useful by-product of the process was the construction of a new extension to the workshops courtesy of the timber provided by the American packing cases.

Then in 1941 a contract was awarded that would have major repercussions within the Nuffield Organisation and in turn affect the very future of the MG marque. Kimber had secured a deal to construct the frontal section of a new bomber – the Armstrong-Whitworth Albemarle – however, company vice-chairman Miles Thomas, who had taken over after the death of Oliver Boden, was less than happy. He wanted to see the group working under his strict control and, as he saw it, here was Kimber acting the maverick and doing his own thing! Kimber was called to task and summoned by Thomas. In a brief meeting Thomas explained that as it seemed that Kimber was determined to work under a policy of non-conformity he would have to go. There were no ifs and buts. After 20 years as the driving force of MG he was out.

MG continued with their war contracts under the guidance of Propert until early in 1945 when it became obvious that the tide in Europe had turned and that it was just a matter of time before fighting ceased. In these final years of war their work included the building of Crusader tanks and the vital construction of wading equipment for heavy armour in preparation for the 1944 D-day landings.

Sadly, Kimber was unable to witness the end of the war. Upon leaving MG he took a job first with Charlesworth Coachbuilders and then, in 1943, with the Specialloid Piston Company. Whilst travelling to Peterborough for business on the evening of 4 February, the train he was travelling on came to a halt in a tunnel just outside London's King's Cross station having slipped on a newly laid stretch of rail. In the darkness the driver was unaware that the train had started slipping back down the gradient. In desperation to avert a collision a signalman changed the points but it was too late. The final carriage in which Kimber was travelling was already half way across and the carriage became derailed to be pushed backwards on its side until sliced in two by a metal gantry. Two people died in the crash that day, one of these was Cecil Kimber.

ABOVE Matilda tanks that were overhauled by MG during the war

Chapter 8

Recovery

DESPITE THE CESSATION OF HOS-tilities on 15 August 1945 it was to be a long time before Britain would return to what would have been considered a state of normality. Whilst it was true that the general public and demob-happy ex-servicemen were keen to return to the life they had known before the war, the economic reality of six years of conflict continued to hit home. Rationing and restrictions remained in force and many goods were constantly in short supply. These restrictions impacted upon industry just as they did the man on the street. With the home economy in tatters the message was clear to one and all – export or bust.

The MG factory was as keen as any-body to get back to business but steel was a commodity in perilously short supply and only allocated in direct pro-portion to the level of export sales

achieved. The company's pre-war sales had been almost exclusively in the United Kingdom. A few cars had made their way abroad here and there but there was no overseas market to boast

the V8 gas guzzling behemoths that were filling the streets and highways of the United States? But the little MG was to prove as popular with the Americans as it had done in the UK.

The decision was taken that, in order to capitalise on essential resources and simplify production, a single motor car would be produced. After a brief period of consultation and design, production recommenced late in 1945 centred upon the TC Midget. Whilst essentially the same vehicle as its short-lived TB predecessor, it featured several modifications. The body was made four inches wider, improving roominess, but to maintain the same overall width of 4ft 8in the fenders and running boards were narrowed (easily identifiable by their two rubber grips instead of three), the rear sliding trunions that had been cause for

of. In fact, in the biggest world automotive market, the trend was for an altogether different kind of car. How could the small sports car manufacturer from Abingdon-on-Thames compete with complaint on pre-war machines were replaced with rubber bushes and the two 6v batteries were removed in favour of a single 12v model. Limited general supplies resulted in early models being available only in black although as production settled red or green were also an option. Some 1,500 machines were built in the first year with one-third of those being exported.

With stateside sales burgeoning, it became apparent that the TC needed to become more tailored to the US market. Although not making a concession to left-hand drive, latter models did, however, incorporate relay-operated sidelight and taillight indicators and a two-tone horn whilst new American vehicle regulations were complied with by the addition of front and rear bumpers and redesigned, smaller headlamps.

The success of the Midget led the way for the introduction of a second car into the MG range but, whereas the TC was a hangover of the pre-war sportsters, this latest machine was an altogether modern affair completely on-trend with the automotive developments of the day. It did, however, maintain roots from deep within the Nuffield empire.

When launched, the new YA saloon retailed at £575. The welded box-section chassis was based on a design originally destined for the replacement of the ageing Morris Ten and created by engineer WJ "Jack" Daniels and Alex Issigonis, a

partnership that would, in later years, create the iconic Morris Minor and the BMC Mini. Although the majority of the bodywork pressings including the bonnet and doors were from the Standard E and the Morris 8, the boot, wings and running boards were bespoke

items built for the MG by the Morris body shop. A beautifully specified interior with leather and walnut trim was gorgeously set off by the use of octagonal instrument surrounds. Handling was much improved over previous saloon models thanks to the introduc-tion of rack and pinion steering and coil-sprung independent front suspension. Power was provided by a single carburettor version of the 1250cc TC Midget engine known as the XPAG.

An open-top four-seater version of the Y-type was released in 1948.

Designated the YT, it was priced the same as the YA but was only available as an export model. A far from appealing car, its production lasted for just over a year before it was withdrawn having sold less than 1000 units. At about the same time the TC was discontinued but its sales performance had been somewhat more auspicious – in its four years of existence exactly 10,000 cars had been produced of which 6592 were exported with 2001 of these ending up in the US.

Buoyed by this international success it was decided that the TC replacement should be designed with foreign markets in mind from the outset – for

by five inches and swept up over the rear axle. To this was added the benefit of improved brakes, independent front suspension and rack-and-pinion steering. A new body was designed which looked considerably more modern without losing the classic lines that had come to define the character of the Midget over so many years of motoring. Once again it was the 1250cc four-cylinder OHV that provided the power. Undergoing little modification it did, however, leave the car a little underpowered, the TD having put on a few pounds around the waist compared to its svelte TC cousin.

If the sales of the TC had caught MG a little off guard then nothing could have prepared them for the unparalleled success of the TD. By 1950, in excess of 10,000 TCs and YAs were being manufactured annually with over 90% of the production being shipped offshore.

With the long awaited end to post-war fuel rationing, a new version of the TD was brought into production in 1950. The Mk II was tuned with competition in mind with a higher ratio rear axle, its chassis modified to take friction dampers in addition to the

a start, it had to be capable of being produced in left-hand drive! The TD Midget took another leap forward for MG – taking the best aspects of the sedate Y-type and combining them with the more edgy, athletic credentials of the sporty TC. The chassis was effectively that of a Y-type, shortened

existing suspension, larger CU carburettors and twin fuel pumps. With power output improved by over 10% this was far more like the car real MG enthusiasts had wanted to see when the original TD was launched.

Once again, racing was back on the agenda although the prospects of any official MG team were bleak. Harking back on old traditions, amateur racers had rediscovered the delights of the Midget and the TD was rapidly becoming the steed of choice for budding competitors. One such driver was George "Phil" Phillips who, having achieved some impressive results at the wheel of his own custom-bodied TC, had caught the eye of the MG works. For the 1950 Le Mans Phil was supplied a specially tuned TD fitted with a low, sleek body of a design originally created by Syd Enever for the next generation of Goldie Gardner record-breaking cars. The new car was a sensation, its aerodynamic lines helping attain a top speed of 120mph, an improvement of 40mph over the standard machine.

But it wasn't just the outstanding performance of this TD racer that was turning heads – its appearance was absolutely stunning! To perfect its looks

Enever soon enlisted the help of young MG draughtsman Roy Brocklehurst to design a new frame that allowed the driver to sit lower in the body and to the side of the transmission tunnel. From this a prototype was built. Designated EX175 it was hoped that this would define the body-shape of the next generation of Abingdon's road-going two-seat sports cars. With everything going for it, it must have seemed like a fait accompli for the MG team when they presented

the finished prototype to the company management in 1952 but once again there were dark forces at work and it was all change for the Nuffield Organisation.

For some time Nuffield had been considering a merger with Austin Motors. Talks were, however, suspended following a meeting of the managing directors of Austin, Ford, Nuffield, Standard-Triumph, Rover and Rootes (parent company of Hillman and Humber), collectively known as the Big Six. An agreement was made to form the Standardization Committee — an organisation formed to promote the use of common components amongst motor manufacturers. With the eventual collapse of the agreement negotiations for amalgamation started once more – this time resulting in the merging of both companies in 1952. With the new company named the British Motor Corporation, or BMC, Nuffield initially took on the role of chairman but at 75 years old, decided that retirement would be an altogether more preferable option. Stepping down to a role of honorary president, his position was filled by a character known all too well to the MG workforce – Leonard Lord – who, since leaving the Nuffield Organisation in the 1930s had taken a management position at Austin Motor Company becoming its chairman upon the retirement of founder Herbert Austin.

The EX175 project was instantly turned down. Austin were ready to launch the new Austin-Healey 100 to the public and to Lord's mind there was only room for one new sports car in the BMC portfolio. Was this an economic decision or personal favouritism? We shall never know for sure but it was met with utter disappointment by the Abingdon workforce who felt it was a personal attack at the marque they held so dearly. Over the course of the next 12 months the reality of Lord's decision hit home. Forced to continue with TD production, MG found they were trying to sell a car that, compared to the sleek and powerful Healey, was slow and outmoded. The reputation garnered by this dated image only served to paint MG as a

company that was on its last knockings. With customers looking elsewhere in their droves even sales of the reliable Y-type saloon suffered.

The best that could be offered by the BMC board was the permission to facelift the existing TD Midget. With its radiator grille raked back, headlamps faired into the front wings and

lowered bonnet line the £550 TF Midget was first shown to the public at the 1953 Motor Show. They were not impressed. It did not take a die-hard MG aficionado to recognise that the "improvements" were nothing more than window dressing on what was essentially a 17-year-old design.

In a strange turn of events, another MG graced the company stand at the 1953 show. A year earlier a new saloon car had been prepared for the Motor Show. With its 1250cc XPAG engine and Gerry Palmer-designed body it had been intended as a replacement for the now ageing and ailing Y-type. However, management intervention had resulted in the car being re-branded as the

ABOVE EX179 in action on the Bonneville Salt Flats, Utah

Wolseley 4/44. Realising that Y-type sales were dropping through the floor the decision was taken to take the Wolseley, fit the larger BMC B-series 1489cc four-cylinder OHV, bolt on an MG radiator grille and, voila, The MG ZA Magnette was born!

There was, however, a glimmer of

light on the horizon in the form of record-breaking racer George Eyston who, since abandoning ties with MG in 1935 had become a director of the Castrol oil company in the United States. Impressed by the marque's unprecedented American success story he visited Lord and suggested that MG should once again undertake a series of record attempts, on the salt flats of Bonneville, Utah. If anyone else had made the approach to the BMC chairman it is a certainty that he would have turned them down flat but Eyston was another matter. Here was a man for whom Lord had the utmost respect and admiration.

Initial tests were carried out using the existing Enever-designed EX175 but, with its bodywork designed with road use in mind it proved unsuitable for the task. There was, however, a spare EX175 chassis in existence and this was quickly dusted down and put into use. Power was provided by a modified version of the 1250cc XPAG motor, bored out to 1466cc and reclassified as the XPEG. The new car, known as the EX179, was shipped to Utah in the autumn of 1954 and proceeded to set a series of long distance high-speed records including a 12-hour run from a standing start at an average speed of 120.7mph with Eyston and Ken Miles at the wheel. In total eight international and 28 national records were taken that year, the fastest of which was a flying start 10 miles in 3 minutes 54 seconds at an average speed of 153.7mph.

Following the attempts it was decided to fit the enlarged XPEG engine to the TF. Marketed as the car powered by a record-breaking engine it helped to reinstate MG as a credible name with the sports car fraternity. Long overdue, the BMC management had realised that MG stood for something special and that for the marque to survive it would need an injection of something new. Permission was granted to commence development on the TF's replacement and, to the surprise of all at Abingdon, the decision was taken to reinstate the design office. MG was back on the road again.

Chapter 9

First of a New Line – the MGA

FOR THE ABINGDON WORKFORCE the prospect of working on an all-new modern sports car was a cause of great excitement. At last here was a chance to give the world the MG car they had deserved for so long. There was only one place the designers needed to look for inspiration – the record breaking EX175. The intention was to take the car from the drawing board to full scale production within a 12-month window.

Roy Brocklehurst's original prototype chassis needed little modification to become suitable for the road and the TF developed independent front suspension and rack and pinion steering were more than capable for the new car. The Midget's adapted XPEG motor was,

however, deemed inappropriate having already been pushed to its physical and performance limits. Instead, the durable 1489cc BMC B-series four-cylinder OHV already fitted to the ZA Magnette was to be used, as was the saloon's four-speed gearbox. Although hardly the most inspiring of engines in standard form the MG technicians were able to weave their magic and add some sparkle with the addition of a second carburettor and an increase in compression. The result was a hike in power from 50bhp to a more impressive 68bhp – an increase of 36%!

A plan was hatched to launch the TF replacement to the public early in June 1955 and then to immediately take three

of the machines to the Le Mans 24 Hour – a brave test of any car let alone an untested one fresh off the production line – and Abingdon may well have achieved the near impossible in turning the car around within a year had it not been for production problems beyond their control. The new sleek, streamlined Enever bodywork was being manufactured by Swindon based Pressed Steel who were, at the time, experimenting with new production techniques including the use of plastic dies to shape the metal body panels. For all of their efforts this technology proved infeasible and only served to hinder manufactur.

Rather than show an unfinished production car the three Le Mans racers were quickly finished and revealed as the new EX182 racing prototypes. This decision may, in the long run, have acted in MG's favour; softening the blow for the MG traditionalists for whom the marque stood for squared-off bonnets, long running boards and that upright radiator grille. Under the

admirably on the Le Mans tarmac, causing quite a stir on their arrival at the paddock, resplendent in British Racing Green with polished wire wheels, low screen and additional radiator-mounted spot lamp. However, the race itself had a far less glorious outcome when, after two hours of racing, a works Mercedes-Benz 300SLR driven by Frenchman Pierre Levegh crashed after clipping the Austin-Healey of Lance Macklin which in turn was braking heavily to avoid the Jaguar of Mike Hawthorn. Levegh's car was launched into the air before ricocheting off a bank and into the densely packed spectators. At about the same time one of the EX182s also crashed at White House before catching fire and seriously injuring its driver Dick Jacobs. Despite the accident, officials decided to allow the race to continue ostensibly to prevent any further panic and to keep the access roads clear for emergency vehicles. Only when reports confirmed the death toll to be in excess of 80 people did the leading Mercedes-Benz team withdraw as a mark of respect. The two remaining MGs were among the 21 cars that finished from 60 starters, achieving 86.17mph and 81.97mph averages.

At last the production MG was finally

guise of being the Le Mans MG racer it was easy to introduce the sleek radical shape with the minimum fuss and maximum exposure.

Whilst never in serious overall contention, the three MGs performed

launched to the public in September 1955 before being taken to the premiere motor shows in Paris, Frankfurt and London. The name Midget had been dropped in favour of a new designation and so the MGA was born. In a perfectly staged test, five production cars were pitted against a Le Mans racer in a one hour test on the Montlhéry track: the EX182 recording an average speed of 112.36mph with its road-going cousin covering a remarkable 102.54mph. Even the usually sceptical motoring press were full of praise; Autocar and Autosport both making top speeds approaching 100mph with acceleration to 60mph of around 15 seconds, some 20% quicker than the TF. Autosport commented that "if you want one, hurry up and get in the queue" and even their more conservative rival, Motor, agreed that the MGA "must be summed up as enthusiastically as it was everywhere received". This was more than enough to convince the public that MG were back on track and once again making true sports cars.

The MGA was a resounding and immediate success. At just £595 it comfortably undercut the opposition for price (its BMC stablemate, the Austin-Healey 100 cost £155 more before tax) whilst offering equal, if not superior, performance and driveability. Over its first year of production 13,410 cars were produced, over 3,000 more than were constructed during the entire four-year lifespan of the much lauded TC Midget. Of these, nearly 10,600 machines were exported to the up-and-coming United States market. Combined with sales of the Magnette, Abingdon was now producing well over 20,000 cars per year.

By this time, the ZA Magnette had been modified and renamed the ZB.

Externally the reworked saloon was instantly identifiable by a tapered chrome side strip on the front wing and doors. More significant changes were hidden away under the curved bonnet. Larger carburettors fed an enhanced B-series engine with an improved cylinder head and raised compression to generate 68bhp – a 13% increase in power – which, when allied to a higher final drive ratio improved top speed and acceleration. Also available to ZB owners as an option was the ill-fated Manumatic transmission – a primitive version of the modern Tiptronic gear-

BELOW The MGA with its beautiful streamlined body

change found on many luxury cars. Using a complex system of vacuums, servos and hydraulics it offered the driver the ability to change gear without the need for a clutch. However, its fragile and over-complicated construction led to many reliability problems for the few motorists brave enough to specify its inclusion, and it was soon abating.

1957 and there was no sign of interest in the MGA dropping off; in fact, quite the opposite was happening. Production increased to an amazing 20,571 cars with an unbelievable 17,195 of the sportster finding their way across the Atlantic. The nation so used to the heavyweight Detroit steel had taken the little MG to its heart.

With increasing speeds becoming available to everyday motorists it became apparent that the rag-topped roof convertible cars were starting to reveal their shortcomings with drafts, leaks and wind-noise being all too com-

ABOVE The MGA represented very good value for money in the mid Fifties

mon. In addition to working on a new hood design, MG decided to first offer a detachable hard top roof before launching a fully closed in coupé. An altogether quieter and more civilised car, the new slippery shape gave an instant increase in performance with speeds in excess of 100mph being easily attainable.

If records were being broken in sales and export, it was nothing compared to what was being achieved by the competitions department. EX179 had made another successful appearance stateside taking 16 international records during August 1956 including a flying 10 miles at 170.15 and a marathon 12-hour run at 141.71. The car returned again in 1957 and, powered by a smaller 948cc OHV based on the type used in the sedentary Morris Minor, recorded a 118mph average for the 12-hour run whilst returning an enormous 49.8mpg. The icing on the cake for the MG team was a 143.47mph flying mile with driving ace Phil Hill at the wheel.

Aware that EX179 was nearing the peak of its development potential, Syd Enever had once again put pen to paper and designed what he believed would be the next generation of MG record breakers. With a tubular chassis and mid-mounted engine the driver was positioned much further forward than in previous EX cars. In fact, so far forward that his toes would all but graze the inside of the elliptical nose cone of the amazing lightweight aluminium teardrop body – a form so aerodynamic that it created 30% less drag than EX179 and sat with the line of its bodywork a mere 76cm from the ground with the top of the cockpit just 20cm higher still. To power it a modified twin-cam 1489cc B-series engine was fitted with a Shorrock supercharger, an immensely powerful unit designed for use in commercial vehicles. Stopping power was provided by a single rear-mounted brake which, when activated, was cooled by air channelled via a small bodywork flap mechanically linked to the brake pedal. The result was a super-slippery record car with almost 300bhp on tap with the stopping power of an ocean liner!

Enever and his MG colleagues had two clear targets in mind for EX181 as this new car was christened. The first was to

BELOW This MG displays the soft top version with its high roof and large windscreen

break the class F record for 1500cc cars that had been set by Goldie Gardner back in 1939 and, as yet, stood un-bettered. The second objective was to push the record further, much further — and to achieve four miles per minute! To their mind there was just one man suitable for the job: Grand Prix hero Stirling Moss.

After a number of delays, 27-year-old Moss started his record attempt on the afternoon of 23 August 1957. With speed calculated using the average of two runs in opposite directions the records fell one by one; first the flying kilometre at 245.64mph, then the mile at 245.11mph and next the five kilometre and five mile at 243.08mph and 235.69mph respec-

tively. Finally the 10 kilometre was taken at an astounding 224.70mph. In all, five international records had been bettered by at least 20% - a remarkable achievement in a sport where improvements are usually measured in hundredths of a second.

A further boost in MGA performance came in 1958. Finding themselves well in favour with their BMC masters, MG decided to create a high-performance version of the phenomenally popular MGA with a view to once again enticing the amateur racers who had provided the marque with so much pre-war publicity.

The beating heart of this special, the brainchild of the ZA Magnette designer

ABOVE 1958-1960 MGA Twincam Roadster

Gerald Palmer, was a 1588cc DOHC developed from the same 1489cc OHV utilised in the existing MGA. By using this same cylinder block it negated any need to change the chassis or gearbox arrangement – the modified twin-cam unit with its cross-flow head and huge 1¾" SU carburettors instead dropping neatly into place. Dunlop supplied both the braking system and the wheels; the standard drums being abandoned in favour of an all-disc system and the wire wheels being replaced by race inspired centre-locking steel ones with light-alloy centres to save further weight. Other than the different wheels, the only distinguishing marks of this per-

formance model were "Twin Cam" badges located neatly on the boot lid and adjacent to the bonnet vents.

The MGA Twin Cam went as fast as it looked with a top speed of around 114mph and acceleration to 60mph in a shade over nine seconds. With handling undeniably improved, MG should have been on to an instant winner. Its £854 10s price tag, although £180 more than a standard MGA was still considerably less than other less exotic marques of the day and once again the motoring press rained praise over Abingdon's latest achievement. But the car soon gained an unwelcome reputation for unreliability with holed pistons being a

MGA production continued to go from strength to strength. On the back of the Twin Cam project the standard A was uprated to a 1588cc OHV known as the MGA 1600. The increase in capacity generated an additional 7.5bhp. Little else changed with the model save for some minor cosmetic differences such as redesigned lights and optional coloured fabric hoods. A Mark II update was to come in June 1961. With the reshaped cylinder head bored out to 1622cc and the use of modified pistons, con-rods and crankshaft, the engine was stronger than ever producing over 90bhp – an increase of 10.5bhp over the MGA1600 MKI – making the last of the pushrod MGAs as fast and capable a motor as the doomed Twin Cam but without the problems of reliability.

LEFT The MGA Twin Cam's distinctive bonnet vents

familiar problem due to pre-ignition caused by the use of low octane fuel. Despite constant modification by the factory it was not enough to reinstall public confidence. Less than 2000 MGAs were produced before the model was retired late in 1959.

To the disappointment of the Abingdon staff the ZB Magnette was discontinued in 1958. It was replaced by the uninspired Magnette Mark III which, to the indignation of the MG staff, was nothing more than a re-badged 1½ litre Wolseley and was the first of the marque to be constructed outside of Abingdon since the company had moved there way back in 1930.

MG had at last lain to rest the ghosts of its past; the MGA having sold an incredible 101,081 cars in its seven-year life. However, the marque was about to turn over another chapter in its history and one that would see the creation of the most iconic MG of all time.

Chapter 10

Return of the Midget

AT THE TURN OF THE 1960s MG dealers were forced once again to look on with envious green eyes at the Austin-Healey showrooms just as they had done eight years before with the launch of the Healey 100. They were all too aware how Leonard Lord's lack of commitment to the company had forced them to produce an inferior model, the TF Midget, long past its sell by date and threatening the company's very existence. Only with the production of the MGA had the balance been redressed. But now Austin-Healey had something new in their arsenal that served to fill a bright new gap in the market and what's more it was being constructed in MG's own Abingdon workshops.

In its first full year of production the Austin-Healey Sprite, as this new sportster was called, had sold over 21,000 units. The design brief had been simple from the outset – to produce a compact, cheap sports car capable of recapturing the adventurous young spirit that, in pre-war years, had made cars like the M-type Midget so popular. Based on the 42.5bhp 948cc BMC A-type engine, gearbox and front suspension of the little Austin A35 saloon and combined with the pinpoint rack-and-pinion steering of the Morris Minor, the Sprite was the first BMC sports car to be constructed around a monocoque body whereby the chassis and body panels were built as a single unit – rigidity being created by integral box-section members and the transmission tunnel. The resulting package, which had quickly become nicknamed the Frogeye Sprite due to its protruding "pod" headlamps which gave the car the appearance

of an amphibian, albeit a very fast one, was light, fairly quick and immensely fun to drive. However, it was not without fault. In some respects the body shell was too rigid for the size of car – on an uneven surface high-speed cornering could be described as a series of hops, skips and jumps – and remarkably the body itself was without external access to the boot. (Perhaps in these modern days of car crime this is a design feature that should be revisited?)

Word soon got around of the problems and with the vociferous motoring press capable of praising and damning in equal measure, these criticisms caused a drop in sales during the model's second year. The solution in the eyes of BMC was to build a Mark II Sprite which would serve to address these faults whilst giving an opportunity to improve power and handling.

The man chosen to lead the project was none other than MG's own Syd Enever. The creation of a redesigned car created another opportunity for BMC – to use this new model as a platform to create a comparable MG.

This was to be far more than a quick wash and brush up for the Sprite. The same original body shell was used but to this were added redesigned wings (without the bulging-eye headlamps) and a totally new bonnet that cleverly made use of all the original mountings. The curved rear of the car was cut away and a new rear deck welded into place and boot lid fitted. Furthermore, to improve interior space a large section of the rear panel was cut away behind the seats. Even the BMC A-Series motor underwent substantial changes. Larger inlet valves, 1¼" SU carburettors, a revised crankshaft design and raised compression all helped provide an additional 4bhp.

The car was launched to the public in 1961 as both the Austin-Healey Sprite MkII and as the MG Midget MkI – known affectionately by the Abingdon engineers as the Spridget. Although at £669 15s 10d the Midget was just over £38 more expensive, MG owners benefited

from a slightly higher overall specification enjoying the delights of an improved interior, double sliding side window flaps and, of course, the inimitable MG badge and grille.

After combined sales in excess of 36,500 cars, a year later a revised MkI Midget / MkII Sprite was launched to the public. Having had its engine capacity increased to 1098cc and now producing a healthy 55bhp, and the fitment of an improved clutch and synchromesh and front Lockheed disk brakes, the new model, although not designated as a new mark, was much improved in every respect not least performance and handling with a top speed now approaching 90mph.

Late 1962 saw the arrival of two new models in the MG range: the MGB Roadster – brought in to replace the now ageing MGA – and the MG1100 Saloon which, in many respects, was often overlooked, thanks to the success

of its sportier stablemates, despite its revolutionary design.

Over its lifetime the 1100 was produced in many forms thanks to the "badge-engineering" that was prevalent within the BMC organisation, bearing the motifs of Morris, Wolseley, Austin, Riley and Vanden Plas in addition to MG. Designed under the watchful eye of Austin Mini creator Alec Issigonis, and styled by Pininfarina, the Italian body stylists responsible for iconic cars as diverse as the Peugeot 404 and the Ferrari Enzo, the saloon was a symbol of automotive modernity. In its MG guise it was powered by the indomitable BMC A-Series 1098cc four-cylinder motor but, for the first time, it was transversally mounted with twin carburettors and drove the front wheels. The ground-breaking Hydrolastic suspension system, a creation of Alex Moulton, was the first of its kind to utilise linked hydraulics. Referred to as being "suspensational" in the MG promotional film Magic Carpet (notably, with Graham Hill at the wheel) the system allowed the car to remain far more stable in cornering by reducing pitch and roll.

Later in its life the MG1100 with a redesigned body shell benefited from a new version of the BMC A-Series – a 1275cc single carburettor variant designed for the Mini Cooper S albeit in a lower state of tune. For some time the MG1100 and the MG1300 were sold side by side until, in 1968, the smaller-engined model was discontinued at which time the larger machine gained a second carburettor and an increase in power of 7bhp. A final revision of the MG1300 took place in 1968 with the introduction of the MkII – a generally updated two-door model with a modernised interior and a more potent 70bhp engine that remained in the range until being dropped in 1972.

During this time the Midget had also undergone a series of changes and modifications. 1962 saw the arrival of an all new machine, the Triumph Spitfire 4, launched to compete directly with the Midget and Sprite in the blossoming small sports car market. Powered by a 1147cc straight-four this Michelotti-

designed roadster instantly put pressure on the BMC motors, being quicker and better appointed with modern luxuries such as winding windows and a more luxurious cockpit.

BMC's response was the MkII Midget /MkIII Sprite. Strengthened with an uprated crankshaft and MG1100 cylinder head, the 1098cc A-series engine's power was increased 4bhp to 59bhp. Now capable of around 92mph it was at least back on par with

relocation of the door lock and handle which had to be completely relocated to allow enough room for the glass to fall into the door. Fortunately these efforts appeared worth their trouble and the following year sales increased to over 22,000 cars.

Just as the 1275cc Mini Cooper S engine had benefited the MG Saloon so, in 1966, it was to benefit the Midget and Sprite as the MkIII / MkIV variants were introduced. Once again the motor was fitted in a lower state of tune as a means of maintaining affordability but, nevertheless, it still managed to produce a

the Triumph in terms of top speed. Amusingly, upgrading the engine was probably the easiest task that presented itself to the Abingdon engineers – creating wind-up windows was another matter altogether! First the doors themselves had to be thickened to allow enough room for the winder mechanism and the glass. This encroached on the cabin space to such an extent that the door-mounted map pockets had to be discarded. More significant was the

respectable 65bhp with improvements in both acceleration and top speed. Other modifications included a larger, more powerful clutch, dual servo brakes and a completely redesigned folding hood. Once again it seemed as if the Spridget was back on a par with its Triumph rival but, as always seemed to be the case with the Abingdon marque, it was all change in the boardroom and soon MG would be presented with a whole new set of trials and tribulations.

Chapter 11

MGB – An Icon

FOR ONCE IN THEIR EXISTENCE, the MG factory found themselves with the almost unheard of luxury of time when it came to developing the successor to the amazingly successful MGA. No sooner had the marque's premier sports car hit the streets than Syd

Enever and his Abingdon design team set to creating what was destined to become the greatest MG of all time. Whilst automotive technology was moving along at a pace, other aspects of the motor industry never seemed to change. As always, the BMC purse strings were pulled tight shut with the excuse being that MG were not seen as profitable compared to other motor manufacturers within the corporation due to some archaic and thoroughly biased accounting methods used within the group.

Enever's first instinct was to base the car on the running gear of the MGA so in 1957 specialist Pietro Frua, the Turin based designer responsible for the graceful and exotic lines of many a Maserati, was sent a 1500 chassis. However, the resulting designs, although stunning to look at, were considered impractical to

ABOVE 1964 MGB works rally replica

build and unsuitable for the relatively small engine size of the British sportster. A new approach was sought closer to home through the minds of general manager John Thornley and Don Hayter, both of whom had spent a considerable amount of time in the employ of Aston Martin and were familiar with the development of the DB2.

A decision was taken to develop a monocoque – this was increasingly becoming the norm in sports car design and had just been implemented in the BMC-designed Austin-Healey Sprite and its MG Midget twin. Hayter had

already penned an open-topped roadster body styling based on EX181 with the MGA chassis in mind but it was not a difficult task to rework the drawings into a practicable form for an integrated monocoque design. Soon the Abingdon technicians set to work on creating a mock-up which, when viewed by the BMC management, was given immediate prototype approval.

All through this process the Cowley bean-counters were keeping a close eye on the project and Thornley was aware that additional funds over the production budget would in no way

be forthcoming. Here lay the problem. The original plan to build the MGA's successor had been based around the desire to utilise the existing chassis, or at least a variant of it. However, as there was little point designing an outdated machine, things had changed and now a unitary construction was on the cards and with it a bill for substantially increased tooling costs. Unbeaten by the prospect Thornley approached the bodywork manufacturers Pressed Steel who had recently moved from their Cowley base to the new town of Swindon enticed by government incentives promoting the expanding Wiltshire location. Keen to capture MG's business, a deal was struck whereby a large proportion of the set up and tooling charges were to be included in the cost of each body produced rather than as an upfront charge. Without this agreement it is unlikely the car would ever have been built.

With the new agreement in place development quickly progressed. The monocoque soon took form; to the front was a box section consisting of the inner wings, front panel and engine compartment, in the middle a second box comprising of the front floor, bulkhead and scuttle and to the back the boot, rear inner wings and the rear panels. Further box sections stiffened the floor and formed mountings for the outer bodywork and suspension. Initial experiments with a rear coil-spring arrangement were abandoned in favour of the ubiquitous (and substantially cheaper) half-elliptical system that had graced MGs for many years. If it ain't broke don't fix it!

A major decision for the Abingdon team was to be their choice of engine. It had been assumed that the obvious candidate for inclusion was the 1588cc unit of the MGA Twin-Cam but this idea was soon shelved when it became apparent that the motor was forever plagued with reliability issues. A second proposal was to modify the 2639cc six-cylinder C-Series engine used in the Austin A90 Westminster by removing two cylinders to produce a 1760cc four-

cylinder. After considerable deliberation a choice was made and once more it was the MGA's trustworthy 1622cc B-Series that was chosen to star. This itself soon proved to be somewhat lacking in power but, by good fortune alone, it was discovered that there were already plans afoot within BMC to enlarge its capacity to 1798cc in preparation for a new saloon car. For once fate had smiled upon MG, saving them from further substantial and unexpected development costs.

The launch of the all new MGB took place at the 1962 London Motor Show to great acclaim. The press had a field day with superlatives. "Superior" remarked Autocar, "delightful" said The Motor, "the best all-round sports-car on the market" extolled Motoring News. And so it went on. The press and public alike recognised that the Abingdon factory had pulled off something rather special and had created an instant

ABOVE New MGB
exhibited at the
International Auto Show

classic; a true icon of British motoring.

All noted how spacious the new car was, not only compared to its predecessor but to pretty much all of the existing competition. Amazingly this had been achieved in a car some five inches shorter than the MGA. MG had realised that not only were they growing up, so were their customers. Expectations were now far higher than they had been in the past. Gone were the days of rough and ready sports cars. The public no longer had a taste for sitting in a cramped cockpit, being battered by the elements and being aurally assaulted by noisy engines. They wanted the sporting image but with the luxuries afforded to the owners of upmarket saloon cars. So sliding side

flaps were replaced with wind up windows, a vastly improved hood kept the elements at bay and an adjustable seat made for a comfortable ride no matter what the distance. Even the boot had been improved and now offered enough luggage space for more than a toothbrush and copy of the Sporting Life. The MG had truly come of age.

It was not that other manufacturers weren't offering similar specifications to their new models it was just that MG seemed to be doing it a whole lot better. A top speed of around 108mph and acceleration to 60 in 12.1 seconds set it on a par with the others in terms of outright performance. However, this machine wasn't trying to be a race car for the road. Its handling was quick and precise but nevertheless civilised making the B a far more driveable motor than many of its supposed rivals and at £690 it was considerably cheaper with the Triumph TR4 £60 dearer and the Austin-Healey 3000 costing a whopping £895.

The positivity of the press and public was easily converted into sales and by the end of 1963 almost 28,000 cars had been produced of which almost 80% were exported (in most cases to the United States). The following year sales of the MGB increased to 26,542 units whilst Abingdon's total production, including Austin-Healey output, exceeded 55,000 cars for the first time.

As sales boomed across the MG range it was time to deal yet another ace from the pack. Announced in October 1965, this came in the form of the super-sleek MGB GT coupé. If the MGB roadster had been regarded as a good car then this machine was truly amazing.

Priced at £825 it still measured favourably against its obvious rivals but now had the looks that comfortably put the opposition in the shade. Thornley later claimed that this was a car "in which no managing director would be ashamed to turn up at the office" – probably a statement that would ring true to this day. At last drivers were fully protected from the elements and treated to a quieter and more refined driving environment! The beautiful transformation of the original MGB to a stunning fastback had been undertaken by

Battista Pininfarina, the designer who already had the iconic Ferrari 275 and Lancia Flaminia in his portfolio and whose company would go on to create the Ferrari Enzo and P4/5 in the twenty-first century. Although considerably heavier having gained 100kgs in roof and reinforcement, the GT performed superbly with acceleration barely affected and top speed actually increased, thanks to the more aerodynamic profile of the closed styling. The handling also improved considerably as the stiffer body negated any degree of body flex that had been encountered in the standard MGB.

Revisions were made to both models towards the end of 1967 with the fitment of a new, fully synchromeshed gearbox, an alternator to replace the ageing dynamo and a different radiator. For the first time, automatic transmission was offered as an optional extra. Cosmetic changes, however, were minimal and mostly centred around the cockpit and with US safety legislation very much in mind.

For the London Motor Show of that year another model was launched. The new MGC, at first glance, appeared just the same as an MGB or GT but closer inspection revealed a number of interesting alterations and additions to the original design. For a start, bigger wheels and tyres were tucked away under the arches making the car stand a little taller whilst the bonnet now sporting a large bulge across its centre gave subtle clues to what lay beneath.

The engine for the MGC had, unusually, been developed from scratch for the project following a series of attempts to create a large capacity sports car which, like the Spridget, could be sold in both Healey and MG guises to replace the ageing Austin-Healey 3000. The original project had faltered after Healey, unhappy with yet another close association with MG, elected to pull out (a decision that would be their undoing when the big-cc Healey was soon discontinued) but engine development had continued with the MGB body shell in mind. Well, partially in mind. Far from fitting like a glass slipper the resulting 2912cc six-cylinder motor

had to be positively shoehorned into position after huge modifications to the engine bay and transmission.

With 150bhp on tap this was the most powerful production MG to date. Public expectation was high – all those horses harnessed to the sublime MGB would surely create an impressive car packed with speed and muscle? Well, the speed was there with 124mph being comfortably attainable but muscular it was not.

The engine just didn't produce enough low-end torque to match the handling potential of the body and suspension. Whilst far from being a failure of design it simply lacked the sparkle that the press, public and most probably MG themselves had anticipated. Priced at £1101 16s 10d for the standard model and £1249 6s 6d for the GT it failed to capture the imagination and was discontinued after just two years and a

BELOW 1968 MGC GT

total of 9002 cars produced.

An altogether more impressive big-cc MGB was launched a few years later in 1973. Designated the MGB GT V8, it had benefited from yet another BMC group corporate merger and the formation of the British Leyland Motor Corporation in 1968 and the engineering exploits of former Mini racer Ken Costello.

Costello had been modifying standard customer MGB cars by removing the trusty 1798cc B-Series motor and fitting a British built version of the 3.5 litre Buick V8 used in the new Range Rover that was mated to the original gearbox and axle via a larger clutch. The resulting car was by all accounts pretty outstanding with a top speed approaching 130mph and acceleration to 60 in less than eight seconds. Crucially, the big V8 produced a massive amount of torque, about 80% more than the 1.8 litre four-

cylinder it replaced, so driveability was improved immeasurably and the criticisms laid at the MGC unheard of.

Aware of the success of the Costello-built cars the British Leyland board sanctioned the development of a prototype V8-powered machine of their own. This was partly a reaction to the recent release of Ford's new transatlantic-inspired Capri which, from the outset had been offered in variants of up to 3.0 litres. The Abingdon machine once again used the Range Rover V8, although this time it was coupled to a heavily modified clutch and gearbox. Larger disks and callipers were fitted to the front braking system whilst the suspension system was upgraded by the use of stiffer racing springs. To help keep everything in a straight line wider wheels and tyres were specified.

On its release there was no doubting that the MGB V8 was an impressive car and gone were the criticisms of the gutless MGC's poor low speed capabilities.

There were, however, a couple of new issues that soon raised their heads. The first related to the actual design of the car. There was nothing wrong with the MGB shape of course but there was nothing physically about the V8 that separated it from the rest of the range save for the V8 moniker fastened to the radiator grille. The exterior appeared the same, as did the interior. For a car priced at almost £2300, about £600 more than the standard MGB, this was a severe oversight. The reality was simple; MG themselves would have included all the bells and whistles in the factory store given half the chance but it was the Leyland board with their tunnel vision who, as always, held the purse strings.

The second problem was way out of the hands of MG or British Leyland. Syria and Egypt had attacked Israel and instigated the Yom Kippur War which, although a short-lived conflict, caused massive worldwide oil shortages. Pump prices rose dramatically and, between 1973 and 1975, the cost in the UK of a gallon of petrol leapt from 38.7 to 73.2 pence – more than enough to discourage many from the purchase of a large capacity sports car. In total only 2591 MGB V8s were manufactured.

Chapter 12

End of an Era

THE 1970S WERE A TIME OF CHANGE for the MGB, MG itself and the lumbering behemoth that was British Leyland. International legislation, boardroom indifference and questionable loyalties all had a part to play in the fortunes and misfortunes of the proud Abingdon marque. Both the MGB and the Midget found themselves subjected to countless forced modifications and changes although few of these alterations could honestly be described as improvements.

The first real problems were encountered in 1971 when at the behest of the National Highways Traffic Safety Administration (NHTSA), the US government body essentially employed to save American motorists from their own stupidity, MG were forced to detune the MGB for the American market. As is often the case, legislation was being put in place by those ill advised to be making it. Many of the regulations being imposed were less for true safety aspects and more for the avoidance of litigation by motorists involved in accidents who were unwilling to take responsibility for their own actions. Other amendments to the design at this time were more in line with BL cost savings than the desire to create a better car. The traditional leather seats were replaced with heavy vinyl that would bond itself to the driver's skin on a hot day and the familiar wire spoke steering wheel was replaced with a mild steel version with drilled flat spokes; this, however, was soon dropped in favour of a slotted design after a police driver managed to trap his finger in one of the holes

thus immobilising himself and the car!

The slotted wheel was itself abandoned just one year later after the NHTSA decided that it posed a risk to wearers of rings and bracelets and was soon replaced by a similar design in which the slots had been filled. More significant legislation had been brought into place requiring that all vehicles be capable of withstanding a 5mph impact without damaging either the control or the safety systems. To conform to this, outsized and rather unattractive overriders were fitted to the front and rear bumpers. But this in itself was not good enough for some.

California, a state with a reputation for bad parking and setting its own agenda, stipulated that in a 5mph impact there should be no damage to the vehicle whatsoever. This was to have catastrophic implications for the sleek and beautiful MGB and its Midget stablemate. In order to comply with these additional requirements a substantial redesign was implemented that resulted in an additional 32kgs of steelwork being fitted to the front and rear of the car encased in black polyurethane mouldings that added 5" to the length of the car and did nothing for its looks whatsoever. In addition, further US legislation required that all motor-vehicle bumpers should be fitted at a standard distance above the ground resulting in Abingdon's engineers having to increase the ride height by 1½". Whilst this may well have protected Californian consumers from bodywork damage inflicted by questionable parking techniques it did little for the car's handling. The once sorted sportster now found itself liable to body roll and a feeling of instability when cornering at speed. It was though not just the American purchasers on whom these modifications were inflicted. In line with the usual British Leyland frugality it was decided that the rubber bumper model MGs

would become the company standard. The cars would never be the same again.

There was, however, one small point of good fortune for MG buyers in the home market in that they were not subjected to the power restrictions imposed on the American models, once again due to draconian Californian legislature. To fall in line with emission regulations a small valve head and single Stromberg carburettor replaced the standard unit and twin SU carburettors with exhaust gases being subsequently fed through an early catalytic converter. Not only was the US market MG forced to carry a substantial weight penalty due to its hefty rubber-covered ironwork it was also subjected to a 20bhp loss in power.

The body-roll issue was eventually addressed in 1976 by the fitment of an anti roll bar but further restrictive legislation was on the cards as a result of Brussels implementing the new EEC Type Approval Regulations. It soon became apparent that the days of the existing B-Series engine, although well modified from its original form, were well and truly numbered. Without extensive reworking there was no way in which it would be able to comply with the ever tightening requirements regarding safety and emissions. The Abingdon drawing office had been working for some time on the project but the fruit of their labours, the O-Series, was to live its life instead in the more mundane surroundings of the Morris Marina and Austin Princess engine compartments.

MG pressed on with production of the MGB and Midget despite it being thoroughly clear that both machines were now way past their respective sell by dates. The 1980s were approaching and they had been in production for the best part of 20 years with their origins stepping back even further; it was after all in 1951 that George Philips' special bodied Le Mans TD inspired the MGA and in turn the MGB designs. There were also new competitors in the market for the crown of affordable sportster: Triumph, a competitor from within the BL stable, had launched their wedge shaped TR7, and a new concept, the hot hatch, had been born overnight with the creation of the Volkswagen Golf GTi. There was no doubting that MG needed a new model and fast.

But funds were not forthcoming. British Leyland chairman, Sir Michael Edwardes, claimed that MG was just not profitable and that the company lost £900 for every car sold; this was despite the fact that the autonomous nature of BL had long since removed the responsibility of sourcing and sales

from the Abingdon plant and that every car built by the group lost money. The writing was on the wall and very soon an announcement was made that the factory was to be closed and the MG marque resigned to the pages of history.

This caused considerable uproar on both sides of the Atlantic. In the UK a mass protest was organised on the streets of London culminating in the handing over of a 12,246 signature petition at British Leyland's head office. In the US, the members of the Dealer Advisory Council offered to place an order for $200 million worth of cars. Even the House of Commons set up an MG Emergency Committee. But it was to no avail. First Midget production was suspended in late 1979 and the factory moved to a two-day working week producing a handful of MGBs, then, finally on 24 October 1980 the Abingdon plant's factory doors were bolted shut for ever.

It was the saddening end of an era, not just for MG but for the entire British motor industry.

BELOW South African-born business executive and newly appointed chairman of British Leyland, Michael Edwardes, outside Leyland's London Piccadilly offices

Chapter 13

Revival of the Brand

ABOVE Members of staff at British Leyland's showrooms in Piccadilly unveiling the new Metro in 1980

THERE WERE MANY PEOPLE WHO bemoaned the sudden resurrection of the MG name when, just 18 months after Abingdon's closure, it was announced that an edition of the newly launched Austin Metro would bear the octagon motif. Considering the lack of attention and poor treatment given to the brand by British Leyland's management in the preceding years, group chairman Sir Michael Edwardes' assertion that "the MG name is now proudly back on a BL product" must have come as little consolation to those who had been put out of work by his decision to close the Abingdon works.

Then there were those MG purists and members of the motoring press who felt adamant that this was not a true MG but just an exercise in badge-engineering in an effort to make a sportier, upmarket car out of something somewhat mundane and ordinary. But wasn't this exactly what Cecil Kimber had done 60 years before when he started fitting sporty bodies and tuned engines to very average Morris tourers? Even in more recent years the Magnette had shared its design with stock of less illustrious heritage. Indeed, the company had come full circle.

The MG Metro 1300 was in fact a very good small car, or super-mini as the terminology of the day insisted upon calling it. The front-wheel drive Metro's 1275cc transversally mounted four-cylinder engine had undergone a transformation with a reworked camshaft, bigger valves and twin-outlet exhaust manifold helping increase power output by 20%, giving a peak of 72bhp at 6000rpm. The car's bodywork stayed essentially the same, the only external changes being the addition of a boot-mounted spoiler, alloy wheels with low profile tyres and, of course, the obligatory deluge of MG octagons. The interior, while based on the standard car, was a thoroughly sporty affair; red seatbelts and

bucket seats giving the cockpit a pseudo-rally car appearance. The car drove well too. Of course this was no MGB but then it wasn't trying to be. The market had moved on and the hot-hatch was the motor de rigueur of the young and trendy.

Although the MG Metro was considered anything but a slouch it was decided to produce an even faster version just five months later. The MG Metro Turbo underwent further modifications to the 1275cc motor; stronger pistons and bear-

ABOVE 1984 Metro Turbo

ABOVE The MG
Montego Turbo –
the world's fastest
production saloon
when released in 1985

ings were fitted as were double valve springs and a nitrided low-friction crankshaft. The key to the additional power was a Garrett T3 turbocharger. Running at up to 7psi it boosted power to almost 100bhp giving acceleration to 60 in less than 10 seconds and a top speed of about 112mph.

Following hot in the tracks of the Metro came two further badge-engi-

neered editions of new Austin Rovers: the Maestro and the Montego, although it has long been rumoured that both were hurriedly brought to fruition thanks to the unexpected success of the MG Metro.

Externally the hatchback MG Maestro was little different to its Austin Rover counterparts save for some stick-on graphics but the addition of twin Weber carburettors and revised porting transformed the R-Series engine from an 81bhp workhorse to a sporting 103bhp gem. One element of the MG Maestro did, however, set it apart – not just from other Austin Rovers but from pretty much every other car on the market. The dashboard made use of a fully electronic display with digital speed readout and a voice synthesiser that would constantly offer irritating advice at what were usually very incon-venient moments. Fortunately for owners Austin Rover had the foresight to include a mute button. The MG Montego was essentially the same car as the Maestro but had a saloon body and was fitted with a modified O-Series engine – ironically, a motor originally developed for the MGB but sidelined thanks to the usual internal BL wrangling. In its MG modified state the 1994cc four-cylinder EFi produced 115bhp.

The Metro's footsteps were once again followed when turbocharged variants were later produced of both models. With 150bhp, the 1985 MG Montego Turbo was, on its release, the fastest production four-door saloon in the world capable of 124mph and acceleration to 60 in under seven seconds. This was soon outdone in 1989 by the Maestro variant which, having been subcontracted to tuning specialists Tickford, topped 128mph.

The life of the MG Metro, Maestro and Montego was cut short though in 1991 as Rover Group (the company having undergone yet another corporate transformation) prepared to release something that was far more in line with MG's sporting traditions.

Chapter 14

A Wolf in Sheep's Clothing

IT IS HARD TO IMAGINE WHAT CECIL Kimber would have thought had he survived to witness the launch of the MG 6R4 in May 1985. One imagines that he would have given his wholehearted approval. After all, he was a racing man at heart and liked nothing more than to see his beloved MGs in the thick of the action and preferably at the front.

Jointly developed by Austin Rover Motorsport and Williams Grand Prix Engineering the mid-engined 6R4 (six-cylinder, rallying, four-wheel drive) was created for Group B rallying – a short-lived class of the sport with little restriction on design and technology that pushed both car and driver to the limits. At its heart was a normally aspirated 2991cc 24 valve V6 with an aluminium block and twin overhead cams situated just behind the driver but mounted in what would normally be regarded as a back to front configuration placing the five-speed gear box in the centre of the car. The permanently engaged four-wheel drive was then driven by twin propshafts providing maximum grip at all times on the winding gravely stages that typified the sport.

Two hundred Clubman editions were constructed to comply with FIA homologation – a requirement that technically defines the vehicle as a production road car – a guise that saw the 6R4 produced as a 250bhp thundering beast. However, a further 20 machines

were constructed to a full international rallying specification. With power in excess of 400bhp these highly specialised MGs were capable of accelerating from a standstill to 60mph in just 2.5 seconds – faster even than the contemporary Bugatti Veyron.

MG's return to competitive motorsport started well with a creditable third place in the 1985 Lombard RAC rally but it was short-lived glory. The following year not a single 6R4 completed a rally – the problems mostly stemming from the overdeveloped and under-tested three litre power plant. Then, after a series of serious and fatal accidents involving other Group B rally cars the class was abandoned by the FIA. Most cars subsequently found their way into the short-circuit Rally-Cross series where they proved to be a formidable force.

Austin Rover later sold their stocks of spare parts and engines to tuning house Tom Walkinshaw Racing from where the 6R4 engine re-emerged some four years later as the basis of the power plant in the TWR-developed Jaguar XJ220 super car.

Chapter 15

A Spirit Reborn – the RV8

AS GOOD AS THE M CARS OF THE 1980s may have been there was no getting away from the fact that they didn't really represent the true spirit of MG's heritage. For years a mention of the marque had drummed up images of open-top motoring along fast sweeping B roads with the wind in your hair and the bugs in your teeth. Creditable as they were in terms of performance, the Metro, Maestro and Montego were really just a selection of mid-priced Austin Rover saloon cars helped along with a bit of spit and polish.

That all changed when in 1992 Rover Group launched the MG RV8. It would be fantastic to say that the impetus for creating this "real" MG was down to the drive, enthusiasm and brainwave of some bright Rover executive who went dewy eyed at the very thought of an MGB but this is, of course, far from the truth. The fact of the matter was that the British car industry had been well and truly trumped by the Japanese when, in 1989, Mazda launched the MX-5 – a small, agile two-door convertible in no small way influenced by the classic British roadsters of the 60s and 70s. Mazda had effectively built an MG. What was even more disconcerting for Rover was the fact that it was selling like hotcakes! Something had to be done and the result was the RV8.

The RV8, however, was destined for a very different market than the little 1.6 litre MX-5. With a Range Rover-derived 3.9 litre alloy V8 under the bonnet, Elm Burr and Connolly leather interior and a £25,440 price tag this was not a car for the traditional 'oily-overalled' MG enthusiast. Its price put it in direct competition with the altogether more muscular TVR Chimaera – a car that, despite the MG's 136mph top speed and 6.9 second acceleration to 60mph, could beat it hands down on pretty much every account – but that is to miss the point. This was for many the first true MG for 12 years and, if traced back to the birth of the MGB, the first new model in 30.

Sales were steady during its two years and seven months of production. A total of 1,983 cars were built of which approximately 80% were ironically exported to Japan. The RV8 may not have been an astounding commercial success but it did serve to tell the Rover management one key thing – that there was still a market for a well built and exciting British open-top sports car.

ABOVE 1993 MG RV8 3.9

Chapter 16

Into the 90s – the MGF

WHEREAS THE THUNDERING 3.9 litre RV8 was seen very much as a retro-inspired celebration of the MG name, there had never been an intention for the big sportster to remain in production for any significant amount of time. For all of its obvious qualities it was, quite simply, too specialist and too expensive a vehicle to maintain year-on-year sales. If after two years you didn't already own one it was purely because you either didn't want one or couldn't afford the £25,000 price tag. It did, however, serve to remind the public of the true origins of this once great marque. The RV8 may not have been the main course but it was certainly a mouth-watering hors d'oeuvre for what was yet to come.

Since the late 1980s and in tandem with the RV8 project, Rover group had been quietly working on Project Phoenix: a design for a thoroughly modern and affordable two seater sports car. In 1989 three British specialist manufacturers – Motor Panels, Reliant and ADC Ltd – had been briefed with the task of creating concept cars within a six month window based upon an earlier MG concept vehicle – the Gerry McGovern-designed MG F16. Codenamed PR1, PR2 and PR3 respectively, it was the mid-engine ADC designed vehicle that found immediate

favour and was progressed to the next stage of development. Although close, it was generally agreed that the ADC design was not quite there, appearing overtly feminine in appearance to many, so after a period of soul searching, the job of refining the exterior line was taken in-house at the Rover Group Canley Design Studio with McGovern at the helm. The requirement was quite simple: it had to be ultra-modern in design and, most importantly, an MG!

Performance was another consideration that needed to be addressed with more than a passing glance as even quite modest saloons were already offering a level of acceleration, handling and top speed way in excess of that delivered by previous sporting MGs. The bar had been raised and Rover needed not only to jump it cleanly but to raise it further still. Ultimately, this was a key reason for the use of a mid-engine layout in preference to the cheaper and simpler front engine / front wheel drive arrangement favoured by others. Aware of forthcoming sports offerings from rival companies this point of difference was deemed necessary

to set the MG aside from others.

When launched in 1995 the new MGF sported a variant of the lightweight DOHC K-Series Rover engine that had first appeared under the bonnet of the Metro and Rover 200 some five years earlier. This unit, with its head, block and sump fastened together with a single set of bolts had been bored out to 1796cc to offer 118bhp in standard trim rising to 143bhp with the addition of VVC variable valve control – a system whereby the engine is allowed to take a deeper breath under acceleration. Keeping all four tyres firmly planted on the ground was a Hydragas linked suspension system as utilised by the Metro – a gas filled descendent of Alex Moulton's Hydrolastic suspension used many years before in the little MG1100. The standard MGF 1.8i was capable of a steady 123mph with acceleration to 60 in 8.7 seconds with its freer-breathing VVC brother taking just over a second less on its way to an even more impressive 131mph top speed.

Lauded for its spritely performance and handling, the pretty MGF was a resounding success with almost all who encountered it. However, some criticism was levelled at the interior which, although well made and functional, was thought to be somewhat bland and uninspired – especially in comparison to the gorgeous sweep exterior.

On the back of this success MG once again decided it was time to dust down the record books and point another of its cars down the Utah's Bonneville Salt Flats. The car in question, EX253, was essentially a re-bodied MGF fitted with a turbocharged 1.4 litre K-Series capable of producing 329bhp which, with its bubble-top cockpit offset to one side and distinctive looks it was as if the marque had been time-warped back to the glory days of Eyston and Gardner! In August 1997, an American speed specialist took the EX253 to 217.4mph.

The following year another attempt was set to be made using an even more powerful car. Big, green and looking like something out of a Dan Dare comic the EX255 was fitted with a 4.8 litre variant of the big RV8 motor. Boasting an astonishing power output in excess of 900bhp the project showed much early promise. However, despite much development work it proved impossible to get the car running properly and, with funds as always at a premium, the project was abandoned without any high speed tests being made.

The MGF road-car, however, continued to go from strength to strength. With the group now under BMW ownership and formally renamed MG Rover a facelift model was launched early in 2002. Designated the MG TF (for no apparent reason!) the redesigned car displayed a sharper, more angular profile with a significantly reworked front end and headlamp arrangement whilst an integrated spoiler was added to the boot lid. Performance and handling were tweaked once more; the interconnected Hydragas system being abandoned in favour of stiffer, more conventional coil-spring units and the introduction of a Stepspeed button shift sequential gearchange fitted to the steering wheel as an optional extra. In its most dramatic guise, the 158bhp TF160 will carry its passengers to 60 in less than 7 seconds taking them to an impressive top speed of 137mph. True sports car performance in anybody's book!

Chapter 17

The Hot Hatch and Super Saloon

MG'S LAZARUS-LIKE EMERGENCE from the grave continued apace in the twenty-first century with the launch in 2001 of three hot saloons based on the popular Rover 25, 45 and 75. Under the auspices of BMW ownership the company had consciously steered away from anything other than the manufacture of pure sports cars – the reason being that any such machine would potentially meet the Bavarian's own branded fare head to head. However, everything changed in May 2000 when the German company decided to break up the group. Having retained Mini for itself, Land Rover was sold to Ford and the remainder of the operation, including MG, to Phoenix Venture Holdings.

MG's new cars – the ZS, ZR and ZT – were more than a cursory re-badging exercise and transformed the functional, but nevertheless mundane Rovers out of all recognition.

Handling and performance were the watchwords of the MG engineers with all three models benefiting from uprated, lowered stiffer suspension. In addition, each engine was tuned for maximum performance and instantaneous response and fitted with a short-shift gear change and lower final drive ratio to improve acceleration.

The cars are as sporty to look at as they are to drive with colour-coded front and rear spoilers, side skirts and alloy wheels whilst inside body-hugging

sports seats and white dials add to the racy feel. Just in case you happen to forget what you are driving a bold MG octagon dominates the steering-wheel boss in all its glory.

Available as a three or five-door hot hatch, the ZR was offered as a 103 bhp 1.4 litre twin cam (ZR 105), a sportier 117bhp 1.8 litre (ZR 120) and a blistering 16-valve 1.8 litre VVC that pro-

ABOVE An MG-ZS in action at the British Touring Car Championships

duced 160bhp and was capable of 131mph and 7.4 second acceleration to 60. Slightly more at odds with MG's athletic image was the inclusion of a ZR turbo diesel. The image of an oil-burner in the range might not have appealed to purists of the marque but with 9.1 second acceleration to 60 and a top speed in excess of 115 mph this was no slouch and was, in fact, quicker than the much lauded MGB! However, this was nothing compared to the specification of the ZR-Express.

At a first glance the specification, dimensions and performance would suggest that this later addition to the ZR range was nothing more than yet another sporty three-door hatch but on seeing one the difference immediately became apparent as it was, in fact, the world's fastest production two-seater van!

Slightly more refined was the ZS. Taught and punchy, this mid-sized saloon answered the sporting dreams of many a company car driver. Customers were offered a choice of four engine variants in either four-door saloon or five-door hatchback bodywork. Even in its basic 1.6 litre 16-valve form the ZS offered 109bhp, a top speed approaching

120mph and sub 10 seconds acceleration to 60mph but this was nothing compared to the stunning MG ZS 180. Powered by a 177bhp 2.5 litre V6 and built around the best handling chassis in the MG Rover stable it was capable of 0-60mph in just 7.3 seconds and a top

its ZTT estate-bodied brother. As was the norm, a variety of engine derivatives were offered with the most basic of these being the 1.8 litre ZT 120. The most tantalising, however, was the ZT 260. With a 4.6 litre V8 under the bonnet producing about 260bhp, the performance statistics were nothing short of amazing. With a roar like a NASCAR racer and huge squeal of tyres thanks to a titanic 410Nm of torque, this car will happily propel you past 60mph in 6.2 seconds on its way to an electronically limited top speed of 155mph. A car truly worth the honour of the MG octagon!

speed of 139mph. A storming car to drive, its road success translated well onto the race track in the hands of the WSR and Atomic Kitten teams in the British Touring Car Championship.

The undoubted flagships of the range were the MG ZT four-door saloon and

With the MG-TF selling well and the Z-cars adding practicality and style to the range the future might have appeared rosy for MG. As had so often been the case in the past, time was soon to tell a different tale.

Chapter 18

The MG Supercar

IF EVER AN MG LOOKED AS IF IT had just rolled straight off of Brands Hatch or Silverstone and straight onto a dealer forecourt it was the MG X-Power SV. Bold, stunning, a statement of brute

power; the philosophy of this unique supercar is hard to pin down. But this piece of automotive drama on four wheels couldn't have a more untraditional MG background.

To trace the lineage of this thoroughbred we first have to start at the 1996 Geneva Motor Show where, looking quite different, it was exhibited as a De Tomaso concept car – the Bigua. Production of the Bigua commenced in 2000 at the company's Modena factory but soon ran into trouble due to difficulties with business partner Qvale Automotive, an American importer of European sports cars. The dispute resulted in Qvale taking over the rights to the car and the renaming of it as the Mangusta. However, two years later and with Qvale experiencing financial problems, having sold only 272 cars, a buyer was sought. For MG this appeared a

good opportunity – here was a finished supercar that already had acquired type approval for both the European and the more stringent US markets.

On acquiring Qvale's rights and factory the decision was made to give the car an aesthetic overhaul at the hand of Peter Stevens whose portfolio included the Mclaren F1, Jaguar XJR15 and the MG Z saloons. The resulting ultra-light-weight carbon fibre body was stunning. This was not a pretty and sleek Italian-

LEFT AND ABOVE The MG-X Power SV-R – taking the marque into supercar territory

ite bonnet of the first lurked a thundering 4.6 litre V8 based on a unit developed for the iconic Mustang and reworked by American tuning specialists Roush Performance. For many its 320bhp, 5.3 second 0-60mph and top speed of 165mph would have been more than enough but there are some people who just can't get enough of a good thing. For them there existed an even more vicious beast – the MG SV-R. With its 5.0 litre quad-cam alloy V8 tuned by Sean Hyland Motorsports in Canada, 385 back-breaking bhp would propel the tonne and a half monster to 60mph in 4.9 seconds from which it would travel at near warp acceleration to an electronically limited top speed of 175mph.

With all that power, the massive Brembo disk brakes, the huge 18" rims and 265/40 profile rear tyres and the deep bucket seats one might think that the SV was too much of a car for mere mortals to drive but that could not be further from the truth. It is immensely powerful but it is power

styled Ferrari wannabe, nor was it the walnut, leather and Savile Row suit stylings of an Aston Martin or Jaguar. This was something that looked half NASCAR and half Mad Max.

Two versions of the MG X-Power supercar were built. Under the compos-

with balance, poise and handling and when push comes to shove it is probably an easier car to drive than the good old MGB. Compared to other offerings from the MG stable, Cecil Kimber might well question its origins but there is no doubt that he would not have questioned its spirit.

With the SV and SV-R, MG at last had a world class supercar in its ranks.

This, coupled with the superb Z sports saloons and the popular and affordable MG-TF roadster, would have you think that the company was once again in good shape. It was however, not long before the much troubled company would once again enter a dark chapter in its long history and one which might well signal the ultimate demise of the octagon.

BELOW With 385BHP the SV-R is the most powerful production MG of all time

Chapter 19

The End of the Road?

RIGHT A protest plaquard in Whitehall as part of a demonstration against the possible closure of the Longbridge Rover plant, April 2005

ON 7 APRIL 2005 PRODUCTION OF all MG Rover cars was suspended indefinitely. The following day an announcement was made to the press that Messrs Powell, Lomas and Hunt had been appointed joint administrators of MG Rover Group Limited. The company was bust.

Just over three months later the assets of MG Rover Group were purchased by the Chinese car giant Nanjing Automobile Corporation for £53 million after a three-way bidding war with Shanghai Automotive and a small British consortium headed up by businessman David James called the Kimber Group.

Positive news came in February 2006 when Nanjing agreed a 33-year lease on the British Longbridge plant and announced its plans to resume MG-TF production. This road to recovery has been long and arduous but journey's

ABOVE The end of an era or a new beginning?

end is now in sight. After two years of inactivity at the West Midlands site, test production resumed early in 2007. With fullscale manufacture commencing that April it is planned that an initial output of 3000 cars per year will rise to 9000 by the end of the decade.

MG has been down more than once but never quite out and each time it has risen to even greater heights. Let's hope that the future will bring more great cars, more great records and a legacy worthy of Cecil Kimber and the octagon badge.

Also available

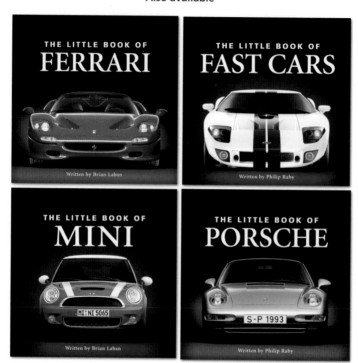

Available from all major stockists or online at:
www.greenumbrellashop.co.uk

The pictures in this book were provided courtesy of the following:

KEITH ADAMS
Motoring Writer

NEIL BRUCE
www.brucephoto.co.uk

JON STROUD

GETTY IMAGES
101 Bayham Street, London NW1 0AG

© BRITISH MOTOR INDUSTRY HERITAGE TRUST

Book design and artwork by Newleaf Design

Published by Green Umbrella Publishing

Publishers Jules Gammond & Vanessa Gardner

Picture Research by Ellie Charleston

Written by Jon Stroud

With special thanks to:
MG Car Club
Motor Industry Heritage Centre, Gaydon
John Pulford – Curator of Collections & Motoring, Brooklands Museum
Mark Hamilton – H&H Classic Auctions
Trevor Williams – Cowley Local History Society